I AM THE CHOSEN ONE

CHOSEN ONE

HOW TO OWN YOUR UNIQUE PATH
& BREAK GENERATIONAL CHAINS,
FROM MISFIT TO MASTERY | REDEFINE YOUR LEGACY

TANUSHREE SAHA

ABOUT THE AUTHOR

I have lived life in various phases. In the first half of my life I have been a designer and a musician. I would consider myself very privileged to have received the best form of education in the country and to have worked in a few of the most competitive organizations to gather experience. I have been a designer by qualification, a post graduate from NID, India. And people also know me as a vocalist, music producer and live performer all over. For the past seven years I have performed in over 500+ live shows.

But this is the second half of my life where I have realized a different side to myself. I always felt a strong connection to the Divine since birth which I have spoken about in detail in the book. And this connection to the source has yet again transformed my life and has led me to choose a different profession, a different industry where I can reach more people who need to hear me. I am not very close to my blood family, due to them making me a scapegoat for their problems. And since the disconnect with them I have dedicated myself to intensive mental, psychological, and spiritual soul-searching.

As a psychospiritual writer, educational speaker and intuitive guide, my mission is to help others find love, strength and inner light in even the darkest of places. I am an inspirational speaker who also delivers channeled messages from the source and guidance that I receive intuitively from the spirit with an intention to uplift the collective. Even as a child or a young adult I have always felt the nudge of a greater calling on the brink but I have been actively pursuing this path since the last 5 years and have been able to help many who have come in contact with me.

This book is a culmination of all my learnings, understanding and derivations which I am passing down to the younger generation who are or will go through a similar journey of knowing themselves. Which is why I have included real anecdotes and stories from my life so that the reader can immediately identify with the pattern and recognize where they stand on their journey. I am extremely hopeful that this book will come into alignment with its sought out readers and help them overcome specific difficult situations and teach them how to deal with people, places and circumstances as they keep moving forward on the Chosen One's predicament.

ACKNOWLEDGEMENT

I would like to thank all the people and their content that I came across on various online platforms like Youtube, Medium, Quora etc which opened my eyes to huge revelations about myself which has ultimately led me to write this book. There are innumerous content creators that I have watched over the last 5 years but these are a few channel names and writers that I will mention, Ryan Tate from Kingdom Protocol, Annie Wright, Aastroind, 111 Shiv Bhakti, Nitty Gritty with Dr. Neeti Kaushik, Nicole Inspired, Sam the Illusionist, Denzo Mos Breaking Empaths Free, Jennifer J. Lehr, Aletheia and Kenneth Garcia.

I would love to thank the entire tarot community on Youtube for uplifting the collective with life saving personal messages and energy updates regularly and helping each individual navigate and overcome the challenges thrown by life. I will mention a few tarot channels that have been very instrumental and have played a huge part in my transformation during the last 5 years. They are Light, Lunar Light Tarot, The Owls Intuition, 144 From the Stars Tarot, Blue Gem Tarot, Jayleen's Tarot Show, A Seer's World, Love Exists Collective, Tarot Yogi, Earth Angel Energy, I Heal Tarot, Led by Heart, White Feather Tarot, Magi got the T, Tunnel Vision. Thank you so very much for all of your massive unwavering spiritual efforts.

Nonetheless, I want to thank Mr. Som Bathla Sir, who has guided us very passionately and humbly with patience on this Author-prenuer journey. He has cracked the code for all authors who want to excel in this industry and made it simple for us to follow this path. I am extremely grateful to be a part of the AFH community, for the constant support, problem solving and well wishes that each member receives. Without the AFH community completing and publishing this book would have not been possible.

I also want to thank Mr. Sooraj Achar for extending his generous help in editing the manuscript and providing relevant suggestions and advice for the publishing requirements.

I thank my parents and brother for playing their part in my life which has indeed made me who I am today. I honour them as my family by birth and wish them divine blessings in this life and their after life.

Thank you GOD for making everything happen in its divine timing

Last but not the least, thanking my profound dog for always being there for me through thick and thin. **'Thank you so much Jerry........ You are the Best..... '**

DEDICATION

This book is a dedication to all the Chosen One's, empaths, healers, intuitive readers, narcissistic abuse survivors, generational curse breakers, ancestral pattern breakers, starseeds, lightworkers, interdimensional messengers, white witches, alchemists, high priests and priestesses and earth angels. I want to honor each and everyone who resonates with these labels or are learning about them, people who are living off the grid, have rejected the must dos of the matrix, who have seen through the veil and are successfully living a life intune with 5D. People who have just gotten initiated on their journey of self discovery or are already walking the path with righteousness. People who have gone through intense trauma in their childhood, adulthood and have overcome it gracefully while keeping their innocence and purity intact. For all those who have been obedient to the Most High, waited patiently for their turn to shine, who have taken all their life challenges as stepping stones to become success stories without losing their connection to the divine. People who work tirelessly everyday to help the needy, sick and troubled people and animals without ever waiting to receive their applause and flowers. This book is an applause, it's a recognition to all those who suffered in silence, worked on their shadow in silence and alchemised their pain into purpose.

This book is for those kings and queens who have been dealt with difficult cards all their life but have divine anointing on their spirits and are destined to be great in this lifetime. I put glory on their name and crown them on their throne as they rightfully deserve.

Contents

PREFACE

This book is a Co-creation with the spirit, Co-creation with God.

This is not mine alone. I cannot take the credit entirely by myself because it's theirs too. It's co-created with them my words of wisdom, my life experiences, and messages channeled from the spirit. I was constantly being nudged to finish this book by them. *Finish it, finish it, finish it!*

Yes.

Took some time to finish it as I take up a lot of different work and wear many hats.

I simultaneously work on many projects in multiple industries that it becomes difficult to focus on one task solely at times. After writing the first draft, I had to take a break. I was moving homes, traveling to distant countries and there were many lives changing events happening at the same time, but I was constantly nudged to finish it because I had to come out to the world. I was being urged to not hide anymore at this point in time. Everything happens at the right time, in the right place, with the right people you know. We call it the 'divine timing'. It was its time. My story was vital, and it needed to be shared, needed to be known by the world. My story had to be heard.

In the last quarter of 2022, I was urged to communicate with my community and share what I know with them, in whichever way I could. It all started because some people in the community who trusted me and liked to confide in me spoke about certain spiritual negative experiences that they were going through, like energy attacks, psychic attacks, etc. They were asking me for help and I did whatever I could to help them deal with it better. Similar spiritual attacks were happening to me too and to a lot of other people I knew at the same time, which made me realize these are all collective experiences and not individual necessarily. A lot of us would be going through similar situations at one time. I was watching a lot of readings and deliverance messages online by various prophets and masters. I observed that one situation would resonate with a huge collection of people at one time as a result of creating a collective consciousness (one body) that we can communicate with. I then decided to help people by sharing information online, knowing it would help them too because whatever I was going through, I was never alone. There was a huge collection of people feeling and living through very similar situations and patterns like mine, as we are all fractals one inside the other, repeating and experiencing the same things of this universe. I started sharing messages in the form of short videos, about things that I had learnt my entire life. Short snippets about various topics, from a life of Chosen ones to Spiritual Ranks, from practising Self Love to transmuting energy, from how to practise affirmations to how karma plays out in your life. I was talking about all kinds of spiritual miscellaneous topics and sharing the knowledge with my community as in when it was coming to me, as in when I was channeling them. And it was at the beginning of 2023 that I decided I need to write this book. Months passed by and I was learning all the technicalities of writing, publishing, and marketing a book. Alongside researching on this topic, gathering all the information from my mind, remembering my childhood, reliving so many memories, trying to understand everything that I went through over and over again, connecting dots and finding patterns.

This book is not an autobiography, yes it has many stories, anecdotes from my life and my experiences, but it's more to do with others. I know I am not alone in what I went through in this life so far; it has been very eventful, very chaotic, adventurous, dangerous yet magical. There are many people who go through a lot more, who have gone through a lot more than me in their life. Some figure out why their life was designed that way, whereas some don't. Some understand why they were called the black sheep, why they ended up there and how their life affected others around them. While some don't out of those, some are trying to figure it out and some have given up. They are too tired and confused; they are just sailing through life, not knowing they are a gift to those around them. They are going ahead with what others have perceived of them, with what others have painted them as and called them. But quietly wondering if anything will ever change, if they will ever know why they are so different, why they can't fit in, why their presence triggers other people. Why is this social anxiety present all the time and why are they so sensitive? They are wondering if anyone will ever understand them genuinely and will treat them rightly. They are maybe being forced to accept the wrong as right, the bare minimum as the standard and the breadcrumbs as adequate.

This book is for all the black sheep, for all those who were ostracized in their families, the outcasts in their communities who were misjudged and misunderstood at some point in their life. This book is for them to understand why they have been given this position and label of the *black sheep*. What actually a *black sheep* means outside the societal norms and familial perception. How to identify yourself if you are one or about to be labeled as one. And how to handle the whole situation gracefully by rebranding yourself as the 'Chosen One'. Because even if you are not aware of it now, you will arrive at that conclusion one day as your life progresses, and I hope this book will help you connect the dots and analyze your surroundings and your life events in a deeper way.

This book is meant to awaken the Chosen Ones, the ones who are called by the divine to carry out a divine mission on Earth, who have a higher calling on their name, who have been called to fulfill a big purpose in their life. They are ordinary looking people with extraordinary skills, talents which could be hidden in the initial part of their life. They are the ones with an unbreakable perseverance, an unstoppable drive, and they are born with an unshakable faith. They have a tunnel vision so clear, their every step is guided by the divine, their will so strong that anybody and everybody around them can sense it. Which is why they get a lot of hate, face a lot of obstacles, and a lot of lies & betrayals await their path because it is so difficult to break them. No matter what is thrown at them, even when the ugliest of the events happen to them, they don't break; they bounce back fast because the divine carries them in their arms. That is the destiny of a Chosen One, who initially is called a *Black Sheep*. Their destiny is so big and the calling in their name is so high, which is why the obstacles they face are also of a huge magnitude. These obstacles are also designed only for them, for their life, because only the Chosen will have the calibre for that, only they will be able to overcome those, it is not meant for others. Others will perish in no time if exposed to such peril, to such danger. Of Course the kind of purpose, the kind of mission that a Chosen is going to carry out will gradually unfold to them, which only the Chosen will know. It can be unique to their geographical surroundings, or a huge world transformative task which is at the global level, or it can be as individualistic as healing and breaking patterns in their own family bloodline. These are some of the common patterns that are seen as missions and tasks that Chosen One's carry out, but we never know it can also be something completely unheard of by the world yet.

CHAPTER 1

BEING THE BLACK SHEEP OF THE FAMILY

A message for all the perceived black sheep of the society, for all those who have been called or made to feel like the black sheep in the family, in your community or in your friends circle at some point of your life.

Now, if I may ask, what do you understand by the word 'The Black Sheep.' Well, google says, 'a member of a family or group who is regarded as a disgrace to it, a person who has done something bad that brings embarrassment or shame to his or her family'.

But in reality, black sheep are people who are marginalized by their family. They are excluded because they hold different beliefs compared to their relatives or act outside of the social norm. Because black sheep are treated differently than the rest of their family members, they often feel sad, lonely, or unworthy. In some cases, the family might even use the black sheep as a scapegoat for all of their problems. Historically, the term refers to the recessive gene for black wool in sheep. Since black sheep stood out from the flock of white sheep (and their wool couldn't be dyed), it made them less desirable to farmers.

SIGNS THAT YOU MIGHT BE THE BLACK SHEEP OF THE FAMILY.

1. YOU DON'T FEEL LIKE YOU BELONG.

Do you feel like the lone wolf, maverick, or outsider? The most common sign of being the black sheep of the family is feeling like you don't fit in with everyone else. Maybe you have different interests, ideas, or beliefs. Or, perhaps you look physically different compared to your parents or siblings. Regardless of the reason, you have always felt like the 'odd one out.'

- Many black sheep move out of their childhood home or state, and they never return.

2. YOU HAVE NOTHING IN COMMON

You're the only one in a family of athletes who can't kick a ball. The only one in a family of extroverts who is painfully shy. You always manage to be different from the rest of your family, each and every damn time.

3. YOU HAVE YOUR OWN LOOK

You don't look much like the rest of your family. They're a little more conservative, whereas you like to show up to family gatherings with an edgy new haircut or crazy makeup. Obscure fashion has always been your bag. You like to change it up and push boundaries instead of blending in with your peers or family members.

4. YOU'RE FULL OF FIRSTS

You were the first one in your family to get tattoos, move away from home, come out of the closet or get a super chic hairstyle, and you're always the first to speak your mind. Your family thinks you're wild or impulsive, and you just don't care.

5. YOUR PARENTS TREAT YOU DIFFERENTLY THAN YOUR SIBLINGS

Sometimes, the child who has the least in common with their parents will be chosen as the black sheep of the family. The parents might not know how to accept and cope with their child's differences, so they use that as a reason to outcast them. Unfortunately, this behaviour can spread to siblings and other family members who learn by example.

- The black sheep are often punished more harshly for the same wrongdoing as their siblings.

6. YOUR FAMILY PROJECTS THEIR PROBLEMS ONTO YOU

If your family members point to you when things go wrong, you're most likely the black sheep of your family. Since you're already an 'outsider,' they don't feel bad for projecting their negative energy onto you, and blaming you, allow them to avoid accountability for their actions.

- For instance, if the parents of the black sheep are divorced, one parent might blame the black sheep for the divorce.

7. YOU FEEL EXCLUDED AT FAMILY FUNCTIONS

Are you frequently left out of family photos? Or are you always the last one in the loop to hear family news? If so, it could be a sign that you're the black sheep of the family. You may dread holidays and reunions because you're often blocked from conversations, or because other family members bring up humiliating stories from the past.

- Many black sheep tend to avoid family gatherings because it causes them stress and anxiety.

8. YOU'RE ALWAYS THE LAST TO BE INVITED

If there's a family outing, you're the last invited ... if you're invited at all. Your family doesn't make it a secret how they feel about you, yet they try to make it look like they truly care about you to outsiders. However, outsiders can even tell that your family ostracises you.

9. YOUR FAMILY TALKS NEGATIVELY ABOUT YOU

Another common sign of a black sheep is being the centre of family gossip. Your family members might criticise your attitude, appearance, career, beliefs, or anything else that they can think of. They may insult you directly or behind your back, but you can always count on them to ruin your day.

- Other relatives may even use you as an example for their kids about what not to be. For example, they might tell their child, 'If you don't study, you're going to end up like Uncle Chris.'

10. YOU FOLLOWED AN UNUSUAL CAREER PATH

Your family is full of doctors and lawyers, and you decided to skip college to become an actress. This is the talk of the whole family. People can't quite understand why you made such a choice. It doesn't seem very smart to them, so, during every family gathering, it's brought up in some way or the other.

11. YOUR FAMILY EXPECTS THE WORST FROM YOU

They hold your uniqueness against you. Don't be surprised when your siblings gossip about you. Often, your parents will exclude you from their good favour and fortune, and instead bestow it on another sibling, even if you need it more, just as much, or that sibling doesn't deserve the help.

12. YOU'RE RIDICULOUSLY SUCCESSFUL

Or the flip side, your family is full of major wrecks and there you are a saint, a do-gooder, top-of-the-class, picture-perfect, Martha Stewart-type (without the tax issues).

Your family is jealous of your happiness and success. They shun you for this unless they need you for something. If that happens, then they are all over you, kissing your butt and making requests of you.

13. YOU'RE SECRETLY ADMIRED

You're the black sheep, but many of your family members admire you. They look up to your desire to stay true to yourself, rather than constantly worrying about what everyone else in the family thinks or wants you to do.

You make no apologies for yourself and it's known that you're "just that way." Even if your family doesn't agree with you, they still secretly admire your chutzpah.

14. YOU'RE SUPER SELF-SUFFICIENT

The only way you know how to be is 'fiercely independent'. You rely on only yourself in all situations. You're always the first to stick to your guns and have your own back. You don't need anyone else to stick up for you or your lifestyle choices because you're a self-styled maverick that makes no apologies.

MENTAL AND EMOTIONAL WOUNDS CAUSED BY BEING A BLACK SHEEP IN YOUR EARLY LIFE

Being cast as the black sheep of the family is not a comfortable role. The pain of being rejected, scorned, and even flat-out disowned cuts deep into the core.

As a person who is the black sheep of my birth family, I know how terribly lonely the whole journey is. All the following wounds I've personally experienced and learned to deal with throughout time.

Here are the main mental and emotional wounds you may develop/experience:

- You struggle to relate to other people

- It's extremely difficult to trust people in relationships, friendships, work situations, etc.

- Trusting yourself and your instincts is hard, so you often feel lost (and without an inner compass)

- Emotional commitment is scary and triggering

- You carry big and oppressive core beliefs such as "I'm not good enough" and "There's something wrong with me "

- Deep down, you feel that if someone truly got to know you, they wouldn't like you anymore

- You feel fundamentally unlovable

- You're either overly dependent on your friends for emotional validation or you prefer to go solo and bypass friendship altogether (as a loner)

- Social anxiety is a regular issue you battle

- Your life feels like one big existential crisis

- You grapple with depressive and/or addictive tendencies

This list isn't exhaustive, but I hope I've painted a clear picture.

Being the black sheep of the family ain't no 'walk in the park.' It is traumatising and destabilising. But you're certainly not alone, and this experience isn't a curse, it's a pathway.

NOW WHAT?

Ideally, we should be able to renegotiate our relationships with family as we become adults. (This doesn't apply if there are abusive or dangerous factors involved. We're not obligated to negotiate with people who have harmed us.) I know very few people who have been able to do this successfully.

What tends to happen instead is one of the two things listed below:

- People stay enmeshed and kind of codependent on their family, even while still being treated as an outcast. In other words, they keep taking crap from them, waiting to be treated better. Or,

- They become increasingly withdrawn from their family, to the point where they start to dread holidays and family gatherings. They might rely on them in case of an emergency, but that's about it.

Neither of these sounds fun! But don't worry - you can balance things out by trying the following:

• RELY ON YOUR CHOSEN FAMILY

Chances are, you connect with these people because they know exactly how you feel, and probably have gone through something similar. Commiserating with someone who gets it can be incredibly validating, which is important when your family treats you like you're a weirdo. (Also, why are you practically disowned for not becoming a doctor, but your cousin is a golden child because they're a corporate executive Monday through Friday even though they're trash on the weekends?)

• SET SOME GROUND RULES

It's not all bad! Can you find some safe topics to talk about together? Decide what events are worth attending? Guess what: You don't have to stay the whole time. You can decide how much time you spend together, what behaviours are deal breakers, and when you're ready to leave.

• LET PEOPLE SURPRISE YOU

If you're tired of the same dynamic playing out, chances are your family still feels the same way. Try speaking up about your experience and you might be surprised. You can always voice your concerns in an assertive, kind way, and see if your family is receptive. Just like you expect them to act a certain way, they are probably expecting you to be the same person you were 5, 10, or 20 years ago. If you take a chance and show how much you've grown, it creates an opportunity for them to step up to the plate. (OK, it might backfire the first few times, but give it some time! If you can learn new skills, so can they.)

• BE YOURSELF

The more authentically, proudly, and openly yourself you can be, the less of an effect other people's opinions will have on you. Part of the dynamic is that you are anticipating what your family will say. Let them say what they want. At least you're busy living your best life. Speaking of which...

• LISTEN TO YOUR CHEERLEADERS

We can all name 2 or 3 naysayers who will judge us for a certain choice or behaviour. Don't list those names! Instead, list the many more people who will encourage you, support you, and maybe even join you. If a hater gossips in the forest but there's no one there to hear them, does it even matter?

Yes, being the black sheep can be isolating. But it's these experiences that ultimately lead people to be unapologetically themselves.

SOME COPING MECHANISMS THAT MAY MANIFEST IN YOUR LIFESTYLE

While the pain of living out the black sheep archetype will look different for all of us, what's likely universally true is that we all probably found ways to cope with the pain early on, ways of coping which, at one point, probably served us extremely well just to survive and make it through that experience of being rejected and misunderstood.

However, as with most psychological defences, there's going to come a time when our coping mechanisms, our adaptive ways of being in the world, likely stop working so well.

The 'shadow side' of living out this black sheep archetype can often mean coping in ways that are maladaptive to the healthy, functional, thriving lives that we ultimately want to live.

For example, some coping mechanisms may manifest as the following:

- Perhaps because you felt so rejected by your family of origin, you walled off your heart and developed ways of keeping other people at arm's length so you'll never have to feel that rejection again. But now you're struggling to form a healthy, close romantic relationship despite truly longing for one.

- Or perhaps you learned to take comfort in food, overeating, or restricting, or bingeing and purging to feel 'nourishment' and 'control' that you didn't otherwise feel from your family or community-of-origin and now your physical body (not to mention your health) is suffering because of it.

- Maybe you developed a deep sense of rage and resentment because you were treated so unkindly and unfairly and this has pervaded your life and kept you in a state of chronic negativity and victimhood.

- Perhaps, because your trust was broken early on by people who were supposed to accept and support you, you developed a hyper-inflated sense of independence instead of learning how to be interdependent with others and you're experiencing challenges with your coworkers, spouse, neighbours, or girlfriends/boyfriends because of this.

- Conversely, maybe because of an absence of functional, healthy parenting early on, you developed an over-dependence on others to compensate for what you originally didn't receive, so now you struggle to be appropriately self-reliant and put too much pressure on other relationships in your life to unrealistically fulfill all your needs.

- Also, you could feel disconnected and isolated at all levels from others and from yourself and this sense of loneliness is manifesting for you as a deep sense of sadness and depression.

These are but just a few of the ways this pain, or this 'shadow side' of being the black sheep, may manifest, but as with everything in life, along with a **'shadow side'** comes a **'light side'**. There is actually a tremendous amount of gift, opportunity, and power that can come with living out the **'black sheep'** archetype.

THERE ARE SOME GREAT GIFTS THAT COME FROM LIVING OUT THIS ARCHETYPE

• GREATER PHYSICAL FREEDOM

When you feel or are rejected by your family or community of origin, there may be more freedom for you to strike out, explore the big wide world, and find your true home. The place you want to intentionally set down roots. And without feeling 'obligated' to stay within the immediate radius of your family or community of origin, you have more freedom and choice to do this.

• INCREASED LIFESTYLE CHOICES

When you aren't beholden to your family's, church's, or community's expectations, you have a greater opportunity to craft the life you truly want, not just the one you're 'supposed to have' but the one you are 'meant to have'. You can more fully choose how you want to love, work, dress, worship, nourish, and build a community.

• THE POTENTIAL FOR A GREATER AND STRONGER SENSE OF SELF

When you're subtly or overtly rejected, you may be forced to develop more independence than your siblings or peers earlier on. This can dovetail with an increased capacity for a stronger sense of self if you've had to defend and assert yourself for a place in your family or community. The black sheeps may often have more psychological 'scars', but they may also have a greater sense of self than the other accepted family members.

- ## A GREATER SENSE OF EMPATHY AND COMPASSION FOR PEOPLE IN THE SIMILAR PATH

Pain can create empathy, and empathy can create connection. I think that one of the great gifts of being 'the black sheep' is the opportunity for increased empathy and compassion for so many others whom society often deems as 'divergent'.

- ## A UNIQUE OPPORTUNITY TO FIND OUR 'WOLF PACK'

When we're rejected or misunderstood by those we come from, we have the opportunity to own and use our voice and our deep sense of self-awareness to seek out those with whom we more closely identify and resonate. These folks become our 'wolf pack', our family-of-choice, our soul tribe, a clan that can love and cherish us in a way that our family or community of origins may simply not have the capacity to do.

HERE ARE SOME WAYS YOU CAN WORK THROUGH THIS

1. VALIDATE YOUR TRUTH

No matter what your family or friends say, remind yourself of what you know to be true. If you were cast aside after coming forward about your experiences, they might say you are mistaken or turn the story around. They might even outright call you a liar. To defend yourself against their gaslighting, the most essential thing to remind yourself is that you know your truth, and that you do not have to convince anyone else.

Family members and mutual friends may not always stick up for you against those who harmed you: Try not to take it personally. Unfortunately, when it comes to speaking up, most people would rather not get involved. It is usually a reaction out of fear, or even a lack of understanding. This can be especially true for siblings or people with ties to the family who are still involved in the dysfunction. Those who know the truth might fear becoming the new target. Or they may truly believe that you are harming the family by speaking out. Unfortunately, you can not control their reaction, and it has nothing to do with you personally, as personal as it feels. Work on moving forward by focusing inward and onward. Healing is not only possible but all the more likely after you have validated your truth.

2. INCREASE BOUNDARIES TO PROTECT YOURSELF

Sometimes we may still wish to visit our family of origin. Others of us may choose to communicate only through email, text, or phone. And still, for some, it may be necessary to totally cut ties with their birth family.

Depending on how toxic your family is, you can choose between the above three options. Do keep in mind, however, that keeping your distance from people who reject your authentic being is healthy. To constantly be reminded of your 'deficiencies,' 'shortcomings,' and 'inadequacy' is not good for your mental, emotional, or spiritual wellbeing. Such people only tend to hold you back in spirals of self-abandonment and self-loathing.

Depending on your situation, this may look different for you. You might refuse to engage in conversations that are uncomfortable or attend events that make you feel uneasy. For others, boundaries might be more about maintaining safety. Do not be afraid to end contact if the situation is unsafe for you emotionally or physically, or if there are children involved and you worry about their safety or wellbeing.

The relief and growth that comes from healing are worth any discomfort that comes from ending contact. Unfollow, unfriend, and block on social media so you are not tempted to look and see what they are doing or who they are doing it with. Decrease the common links they can use to get to you like your distant cousin, who they use as a messenger, etc. It's okay to tell them you do not wish to hear any updates.

3. ALWAYS REMEMBER: YOU ARE NOT TO BLAME

Consciously, you may know this, but deep down there's probably still some doubt in you. Sure, you may have made some pretty serious mistakes in your life, but so does everyone. Just because you are imperfect does not mean you are the source of the dysfunction in your family. If you were the Identified Patient (or still are), you must realise that the cause of suffering in your family is their own repressed anger, insecurity, fear and personal and generational trauma which they project onto you and haven't taken responsibility for.

What happened was not your fault, especially if it happened during childhood or your younger years. A child is never to blame for the dysfunctional household dynamics. You were not to blame for traumatic or dysfunctional events that took place inside the home, and you were not to blame for acknowledging or speaking out about your experiences. Others, especially those who have not yet done their own work of healing, will try to blame you for speaking out.

If you are struggling with childhood or family trauma, or learning how to create boundaries in the aftermath of a dysfunctional family situation, look for a therapist who specializes in working with survivors of family trauma and who understands these aspects of family dynamics.

4. CREATE YOUR OWN AUTHENTIC SOUL FAMILY

After being accustomed to a certain role and way of being for our whole lives, it is strange and daunting to consider moving into other roles. But please know that you can have a family of your own and step into a new role that is relational, not isolated. You can move on with your life, find your own friends, make your own soul family and redefine who you are as a person. The only thing stopping you is clinging to the past and not opening yourself up to being more. Practising the art of letting go will help you tremendously.

5. CONTEMPLATE YOUR BIRTH FAMILY'S PAIN

Once you are at a stable point in life, turn your mind onto your birth family. Exploring the "why?" of what happened can help us make peace with our past and close that chapter.

Reflect on what causes a person or group of people to reject or demonize a person in the first place? Sure, they may be narcissistic or stupid, but that's a surface judgement. What's below narcissism or stupidity? Usually, the answer is fear and pain. When a person or group of people need to subconsciously elect someone else to personify their own pain and distress, someone to point the finger at and pin their problems on, these are very unhappy people indeed. They haven't yet learnt how to consciously handle their feelings of guilt, insignificance, embarrassment, or disappointment with themselves and their lives. They are only projecting all their personal disappointments on your life.

By not accepting their inner strife, they are continuing to build a cocoon of hurt and resistance, which prolongs their pain. So essentially, these are people who are deeply and consistently miserable human beings. While we usually can't awaken our families from their destructive habits, we can develop compassion and forgiveness for them, understanding why we were treated the way we were in the first place. It was actually nothing personal. The exercise of understanding this whole thing is extremely free.

6. LEARN TO LOVE YOURSELF AND EMBRACE YOUR WOUNDED INNER CHILD

We all possess an inner child, the part of us that sees the world through the eyes of innocence, wonder and spontaneous joy. Our inner child, however, also copes with the greatest amount of wounding growing up and it's for this reason that we need to learn to listen to and nurture it.

Signs that you have a wounded inner child include addictive tendencies, sudden unexplainable fears, anxiety and depression, and the unshakable feeling of being worthless, 'not good enough,' and empty inside. If you find that no amount of self-improvement helps, chances are that you aren't going deep enough. Your inner child must be sought out, embraced and nurtured through the practice of consistent self-love.

7. TREAT THIS AS A RARE OPPORTUNITY TO DO SOME SOUL SEARCHING

Now that you are largely free of the fetters of your family of origin, you can walk your own path and be a lone wolf. You can turn inwards, listen to the whispers of your heart and plunge into the depths of your soul.

Those who are not embraced by their family of origin often struggle to get to the place where they can turn inwards. They are beset with the pressures of having to live up to expectations, having to project a consistently acceptable self-image amongst other soul-constricting burdens.

Thankfully, you don't have to deal with this any longer. Once you embrace being a black sheep and no longer fight against it, you are initiated into your own unique spiritual journey. What could be more precious than that?

8. CONNECT WITH YOUR HEART AND LISTEN TO YOUR INTUITION

Finally, to heal the wounds of being the black sheep of the family, you need to reconnect with your heart. I know this may be scary. I remember how terrifying it has been for me to do this. But I've learned that slowly tuning into my inner centre helps me make wise decisions and live a wholly authentic life, the kind that many people dream about.

When being outcast by our family, it's common to close the heart and totally shut off from life. This is a wise self-protection mechanism. But eventually, you need to learn to open back up. To feel your pain, to do your grief work. To practise letting go, to blossom into your truest self. Many people overly rely on their family members for guidance. However, because you won't have that, you'll need to rely on the wisdom of your own intuition. While this is harder to do, it is a wiser path. No one can live your life but you. No one can do the inner work of intentional spiritual alchemy but you.

THE POWER OF BEING 'THE BLACK SHEEP' IN YOUR FAMILY

IT IS A TREMENDOUSLY IMPORTANT PATHWAY TO SPIRITUAL TRANSFORMATION.

WHY?

When we are rejected by our birth family, we are given a gift many others in life aren't. The doorway to unfettered freedom. While others who are embraced by their families still need to play by certain rules, black sheep have the chance to walk their own paths. While accepted family members might benefit from being validated, they also tend to be trapped in limiting roles that make it difficult for authentic soul growth and expression to occur.

Black sheep, on the other hand, have a clean slate. The doorway to trailblazing their own destiny is open, they aren't held back by other's opinions because the judgement has already been made, they are rejects, oddballs, and outsiders.

Sure, there are cases of perfect families who lovingly uphold the dreams and aspirations of their members. But these instances are the exception, not the rule. The truth is that most families are dysfunctional. They are products of our wider fragmented society. And thus, they tend to have a stifling effect on one's spiritual path and evolution.

As a black sheep, you are gifted with the chance to do some authentic soul searching, free from the suffocating confines of your family's expectations and desires. You have already been cast in the role of distaste and disappointment. There's not much else your birth family can do to harm you. The wound has already been inflicted. Now, your job is to break free and find your true meaning in life.

WHAT YOU HAVE EXPERIENCED IS IN REALITY, **A SPIRITUAL INITIATION!**

Examples of "The Black Sheep" Archetype In Media and Literature:

Using films, media and books as tools in our own personal growth over the years, I've collected a list of those I think embody 'The Black Sheep' archetype in both big and subtle ways from my own reading/viewing.

- Luke Skywalker from Star Wars

- Frodo Baggins from Lord of The Rings

- Elphaba from Wicked

- Harry Potter

- The Ugly Duckling

- Simba in The Lion King

- Elsa from Frozen

- Maleficent from the Sleeping Beauty story (check out the

2014 Angelina Jolie version for a complex example of how the "shadow" of "The Black Sheep" can manifest)

- Jon Snow from Game of Thrones

- So. many. characters. In Orange Is the New Black, but particularly Piper in the context of her family

- Hans Christian Andersen's The Little Match Girl

- Martha Beck's autobiographical narrative in Leaving the Saints: How I Lost the Mormons and Found My Faith*

CHAPTER 2

MY TESTIMONY OF GOD

This entire book is a testimony of God, of the Divine, for having me survive for this long, for keeping me alive. I guess I will mention it more than a few times in this book because that is one of the main purposes of creating this book. Thank you so much dear Lord for being with me, for doing so much in your power, for protecting me so fiercely, for always watching out for me, for alerting me about every little detail that I needed to know, for standing next to me till now so that I could tell this story to the world today.

Yeah, this is my testimony of God for everyone to know that God exists, that His favor exists and His wonders do prevail. It's only His will that prevails, no one else's. It's His orders that become a reality and no one else's. No one can play God, no human or non-human entity can play God, no matter how much they believe and how much they try. I am saying that because I have seen it myself, how lives of people who wanted to play God have been destroyed by themselves, by their own doings. When you repeatedly disrespect Him and his orders, when you repeatedly challenge His authority, forgetting that you were made by Him after all. It's extremely sad that some people forget that, it's diminishingly stupid for those who forget that and think they are greater than God, because ultimately God puts them in their place very harshly, they learn how small they actually are in a very rude way. They are those people who have very obvious and popular rude awakenings. They are humbled by God time and time again, through unexpected tower moments and shockingly devastating events, everytime they forget their place.

The kind of upheaval I underwent in my life at various time intervals I would have not survived so far. All these past years that I look above my shoulder now and I really have to give Him the credit. He does exist. And just like the good and the bad both exist, the Good Lord and the devil both exist. This is my declaration of witnessing both the energies very closely.

I was kind of brought up in a haunted house where I slept in the lap of the devil every night. I could have gotten killed any moment. But I was saved every night. One night, then the second night, then the third night. Like that, I was saved week after week and month after month until years passed by. They couldn't capture me. The most amount of transformation happened to me in the last few years, where the devil really made it tough for me. They came for me hard. They kept showing up again and again through various ways, manifesting through different people, family members, friends, potential partners, co-workers. It was tough dodging these bullets, but through years of training, which is what I call this, anyone will identify the patterns. I was saved in spite of all odds because the Most High has the final say and it was not my turn to lose.

What I could pick up from my intuition is that the negative energies also want me. They either want my life or they want me to turn towards them. They want me to surrender to them and adopt their evil ways. Something like that. But I never turned towards them, although I have lived with them all my life, experienced them all my life. I have literally looked them in the eye and existed in their presence every day. I have seen them from very close and I have come to a point now where I can communicate and negotiate with them. I tell them that they can live in their territory and I can live in mine without needing to disturb each other. There have been many supernatural occurrences in my life.

How sudden cosmic alignments, the alignment of stars, have occurred just in time to come and save me, to protect me from dangerous situations and for which I know that I am the testimony. It is almost like a miracle.

The last few years have been very rough where most of my transformation has happened. And it is still happening. Right now when I write this page we are under the influence of a total Solar eclipse in April 2024 in the house of Pisces, which is my sign, while mercury retrograde is going on. Extreme energetic shifts are happening at the moment at a collective level all over the planet. Lots of energy exchanges are going on in the universe right now. I am trying to stay grounded, not trying to get carried away by emotions, keeping calm, although it's so tough. I have had to let many connections end during these last 5 years, along with one intense connection which I had kept very close to my heart for all these years. This is how things work in this world. When the universe brings its transformational energies collectively, it's better to give in than to keep fighting against it. Because you cannot escape its effect, it is bound to do what it has come here for. It will shift timelines for the ones who are ready. It will make the changes whether you like it or not, no matter how painful it may seem. I have had to let go, go through tunnels of shifts, jump timelines, change my skin many times in these last few years. I have kept seeing deaths and rebirths over and over again, and with every re birth it was a different me coming into existence every time. I am a Scorpio moon, which means I will have very drastic, intense life changing transformations in this entire incarnation till the end. But in spite of all odds, I am still here penning the words, page after page, keeping patience, sipping water, green tea, whatever I can grab.

It has been quite a challenge. But people who see me, who somewhat know about my life events, they wonder how I have been keeping up, how I was able to come back on the track so fast. They won't always be able to ask me, but it would flash on their faces asking why I don't look like what I went through. 'You look like you never went through anything, like you always had a fun and beautiful life with a perfect family', you know, having the silver spoon in your mouth kind of life, but that is the whole mystery about me.

My classified fact is that I have been preserved that way by the divine till today. The negative people who have tried to harm me multiple times in the last few years, they might be reading this book too, as they always keep a check on me, they constantly watch every update, every post, want to know what is happening in my life, and this book is a life update to them too.

It is a testimony to God.

A testimony for my enormous spirit team in the spirit realm

A declaration for my ancestors, Ascended Masters and Star Family

It is because of them.

It is a representative case for the Chosen Ones,

The anointed ones,

It is a message even for the perpetrators. When God says 'NO', they have to stop.

Or else their entire empire collapses, no matter how powerful they seem.

They lose all their powers, physical and spiritual. If they had a high spiritual rank, they get demoted, their badges removed and placed in a spiritual jail. Their lives are destroyed because of their own karma. They cannot blame it on anyone, it is their own doing.

MY DAY TO DAY INTERACTION WITH THE NEGATIVE ENERGIES

I have lived with negative energies every day. Narcissists, mentally deranged people, and malfunctioning wounded individuals are nothing but the influence of heavy negative energy reflecting on a person in a very deep way. These are people suffering from ancient curses, evil possession, energy manipulation and deep unhealed trauma. Of course, in the modern medical industry doctors will give such things many names, personality disorders such as bipolar, psychosis etc, and schizophrenia, which doctors agree is a generational disorder passed on by parents.

Now, going back to my childhood, I was brought up in a haunted house. I have seen the negative energies from very close, manifesting into mental disorders, hallucinations, suicidal tendencies, murder attempts, etc. in people. I have witnessed them every day in others around me, but not in me. Somehow, they couldn't get the best of me.

I am just giving an example. It's a metaphor, not literal. As a young kid, if you get slapped every day when you are, say, 5 years old or 10 years old, then when you grow up, by the time you are 25, you know how to control that man who slapped you every day. You will no longer let him slap you because you know his patterns. You know how that man functions; you know his weaknesses and you will press the right buttons now to make it work in your favour now. So it is something like that. It is like that kind of story in my life where I sort of had to master a certain energy because it is the duality of life. It is like good and bad and I got exposed to both in very intense ways at a very young age. I was protected by God and his angels nonetheless but at the same time I had to see the evil from very close and which is why even today I am able to spot negative energy, evil in people very easily.

It will not skip my eye. It is part of human nature. We all have it. It's the duality, but it needs to be kept in balance, kept in check. Negativity always comes to our minds. Weird thoughts of harming others, ourselves out of sheer jealousy and hatred, do enter our minds from time to time, but the question is, are we acting on them? If we are not acting on them, these energies as thought forms will slowly stop coming. The frequency of these energies will reduce. That is how you keep them balanced. If we act on them, we are going out of balance and we will need to remember that we are inviting more negativity and destruction in our own life also, not just for others. The choice is ultimately ours.

I try to protect anyone who I see in danger, especially little children or animals or under-privileged young women, because if anything really wrong happens when they are very young, they won't be in their power to protect or defend themselves. They are extremely vulnerable and helpless. They can even lose their life sometimes or end up getting damaged beyond repair if not helped at the right time. I was protected in that way, but everybody else might not be privileged like that. Every time I see someone needing help, I see myself in them. It's like me trying to rescue the younger me from the past and healing the inner child. It's a very emotional and intense feeling.

Even my distant family, like my distant cousins, aunts and uncles, are quite unaware of what was going on in our lives. They will get a shock if they happen to read this book, after going through the details in my book because they have only heard one side of the story. Whatever they have been told all these years is from the perspective of the elders, basically my parents, and that is all they are aware of. But this is from my perspective, this is from my eyes, what I have seen. For the first time, it has been narrated from my perspective, from my eyes, it's my world. What I have seen, how I have witnessed it.

I am putting out that version of the story. So naturally, it might come out as a complete revelation for them.

THE ENEMY CAME IN ALL SHAPES AND FORMS

They came in all forms.

They were all devil's agents.

They came in spirit form, human forms, humanoid forms, even in reptilian humanoid forms. They tried to take me out many times. They were even in the family, not distant but very close ones in the family. They were attacking from all angles and at different time intervals throughout my life, not just during a single phase. Every year, every two years, every alternate year like that. They kept coming again and again. I was deceived a lot of times. I was also very naïve all those years, just gathering life experience. I didn't realize a lot of things back then. With my heart chakra wide open, I was always very giving and forgiving. Kept myself at the back burner, quite a people pleaser and always thought of others before me. Had a difficult time saying 'No', rarely say No' rather. So they would become my friends. They would befriend me and even become best friends at times, just to take me out. They would become narcissistic lovers, obsessed friends and overly attached acquaintances with a very unhealthy level of competition. But I was still saved every time. I suffered badly during my adolescence, was taken advantage of, and fell into weird, life-threatening circumstances. But all of those encounters taught me huge lessons, and I kept building an arsenal of information at the back of my mind, which turned into wisdom that could change the lives of many others. Gradually I could differentiate covert narcissists from full-blown narcissists, from people who genuinely needed my help, to others who wanted to hang out with me for an ego boost. I was also able to spot the false twin flame, soulmate connections that were sent to me by the enemy again and again, which definitely were so intense, very close to being real, anybody could get fooled but were just there to keep me in a loop of illusion, heartbreak and delusional love. They were trying so hard to throw me off track, shake my focus, or burn my energy out by sending these distractions. It was crazy to have witnessed these games and the level at which it was being played, the very advanced level games of the matrix. I was tested by the universe in that manner. If I passed those tests, I would be sent to the next level. If not, the same test would reappear in a couple of months or almost immediately. They will always give you many chances to improve your grades. The Universe would let the devil fool me till a point, to test my discernment, my emotional intelligence and if I really meant it when I said my self love was on point. But I would always receive alerts when the danger got heavy, or I needed divine help, because hello, this is what we call training. I am only getting trained for the next levels. The universe won't let me get scratched beyond play fight. After all that I have seen and been through, it has to get used in the next phase of my life.

This message is for all the **Chosen Ones**. The enemy knows who you are. They know about each one's overall destiny. They might not know the details and the exact change that you are here for, but they know what you are capable of. What skills are you being born with? Which is why they don't take it lightly. They are after you from the time you are conceived in the womb; they are very scared of what you will bring when you come of age. They will remain very close to you, watch you, interrupt your life, stop you from blooming, or end your life. When they fail to do so, they send monitoring spirits to find out the real details, your future plans etc just so they can ruin it for you or divert your attention to something completely unnecessary. In that way, you lose your motivation and miss the time frame in which you are supposed to complete your assigned tasks.

The **enemy** knew who I was even before I knew who I was. He knew me as a baby. Right? We have a very close relationship. So, knowing me and knowing my weaknesses, knowing my personality, they kept sending all kinds of temptations and attachments to attack me, thinking that I would get lured in. In my younger years I even gave into some of those worldly temptations not knowing how much it would harm me, not seeing everything through, not valuing what I had but only chasing the temptations like a wild horse without looking at the collateral damage and not having understood God enough. I even hurt people but I had to pay a huge karmic balance since then. Maybe I am still paying for that. It taught me how real karma is. But, thankfully, I accepted my faults, my shortcomings and tried improving myself every day in a genuine way. Over the years, it has become a passion to live as the best version of me, not just in the worldly sense but in the eyes of the divine, to embody my highest self. I really wanted to please God after that, not people anymore.

After everything God has done for me, I owe Him that bit.

It's all thanks to Him, for everything that I am today.

I've seen way too much, learnt about myself and the secrets of the universe. It feels like the training is mostly over. The arsenal is full. It's stocked with heavy weaponry now. It needs to be used in the world.

Because there is this force above my head, this power above my head, which just won't

Let me interact with negative energy anymore. It won't let anything delay my purpose anymore. I've been saved and kept hidden for a long time, to avoid any further karmic entanglements, unnecessary energy drainage and, of course, to hide from the enemy and its agents. I've been in isolation for many years now, around 5 yrs with minimal contact with the world, mostly online. It's not easy, living in a city and curbing your social life to null. It got very frustrating; I thought it would end after a couple of years, but it only got much more intense. I kept shedding all kinds of energies, people, places, jobs, hobbies, identities over the years until there was none left of the old. All the old energies vibrating at the old frequency had to leave, preparing and making space for everything new. I sort of stopped resonating with everything old for real. Even if I tried holding onto some of the dearest people, it just didn't make sense anymore. I used to find those people very interesting to spend time with and have interesting conversations matching my intellect. But even those one or two people became completely irrelevant, to my utter surprise. It was like one fine day I woke up and these people were not my match anymore. I had some epiphanies and realised I had again made a huge jump. I peacefully let them go, without much drama. By now, I had mastered the art of letting energies go. I had jumped timelines many times, did quantum jumps several times, everytime I underwent formal healing sessions, I would shed so much baggage and step into a new energy, a new frequency. And I started attracting everything new, which is supposed to match my whole new vibe.

BEFORE YOU INTRODUCE YOURSELF YOUR ENERGY INTRODUCES YOU

My vibe spoke to me. It is always like that for everyone. Before you introduce yourself and your energy introduces you. It does the talking before you even make eye contact. And my vibe says this very loud 'If you want to come, come clean or don't come at all'. This is the message I gave out to the whole world without any prejudice.

And even after that, when people tried to approach with wrong intentions, they were stopped right there, not by me but by the divine. They were not allowed to experience my energy or be in my presence. It is like that now, even if the devil comes and lives in my house, we can maybe share a meal together and then say, 'Okay, I stay here and you stay there, let's call it a night'. That is how I have become proficient in maneuvering the energy without surrendering to them while looking in their eyes every day.

It is like the old American horror movies, where they show exorcism. Yes, the movies are exaggerated for the sake of drama, but a lot of it is similar to reality. After all, movies are inspired by real life and not the other way round. I've seen and heard similar kinds of things right in front of me all my childhood. It was practically dinner table talk every day. People under heavy evil possession right in front of my eyes, doing all kinds of evil activities under the same roof. I know it sounds very dark, but it's true. I had to deal with it and live with it, as there was no other escape. My life was going on along with it. I had to do the regular things like other normal kids, go to school, do my studies, write exams, make friends at school and, most importantly, act normal. It was very difficult to act normally.

Of course I was traumatized. It was some huge trauma that just won't leave you until you run away into a different world. It would show on my face because as a child I'm not able to entirely hide it. I was only trying; I was just a kid. My facial expressions were different. I was even asked by other kids, why do I look like Ive seen a ghost?

I was like, what can I say?

I mean, even if I tell you won't even believe me, so it's those kinds of heavy things I had to process.

And it became a normal part of my life where I had to accept it as my destiny, as a part of my life. I had to normalize it.

It is a huge benchmark for normalizing anything, right?

Like the negative energies are there in the other room and I'm in my room doing my homework. I know it's asking for too much for normalcy, but yes, I had to do that because I had no other choice and thankfully I had enough strength in me to pull through it year after year even after witnessing so much on a daily basis.

Because you cannot fit in with anybody when you have something like that going on at home. Fitting in with anybody as such was never my priority, whether it was the college fraternity, whether it was school kids or in general society. I know I'm here to stand out and not to fit in and my life is too much of an escapade for anybody to understand and as we are not people pleasing anymore; we care less to explain everything about ourselves.

Because over here I'm trying to dive into the normal 3D way of life, but in my other times, I'm completely dealing with a very different world of the supernatural.

I have lived a supernatural existence all my life.

80% of my life has been that. So I definitely won't fit in the 3D most of the time, although I try. I'm mostly plugged into the other densities as soon as I plug out of 3D.

My world has been a combination of Disney Princess + Fairy tale + Horror movie + Fantasy web series like Witcher.

I've done a lot of things like that in this life.

It has been a fairy tale, and I have had to slay demons every waking day.

Which is why I don't resonate with the regular world and the regular 3D life.

For people who always wonder why am I so mysterious or why do I have to keep myself so aloof, it's because I have to protect myself in a different way, with a little more care,

To a different degree, because things are not very normal in my life. It has never been. I can predict the patterns, but I still can't be sure of what to expect at times. So I have to keep myself a little detached, stay vigilant of my surroundings and cannot let my guard down immediately for everyone I meet.

CHAPTER 3

MY CHILDHOOD

FINDING PATTERNS IN THE FAMILY

The first seven years of my childhood were kind of smooth, I was a quiet child, spoke only when spoken to, minded my business, too kind, sweet, had an intense connection with animals from as long as I can remember, scored good in school and did get bullied at times for my wide-eyed innocence. The first seven years of my life were peaceful and quite uninteresting, I barely made friends, didn't ask many questions at school, wasn't very particular of a hobby, was close to the maids who lived with us, I would play with them for lack of friends or any neighbor kids of my age. I was happy as we had many animals in the house, from dogs, guinea pigs, rabbits, parrots, chickens and once in a while we also had wild visitors like mongoose and wild cats, etc. We lived in the capital town with all the facilities of a city which also had the charm of a countryside landscape. There were huge empty lots around our house with a pond and marshy lands. Occasionally we would hear foxes howl at night, the rare quail walking around and blue kingfisher birds flying above the pond. I used to be in my own world, very detached from everyone, even at that age. At times I would be so uninterested, I wouldn't be able to follow the rules of games or any sports in school and would quit right after. We moved towns to live in our own house, from one state capital to another, schools changed, friends changed and I still remained the quiet one. Disappearing into my own world every chance I got. I was peaceful with my life, with what I had, did not aspire to many things or compared myself to anyone. Never felt like I was missing out on anything. The world was all ok apart from home though, the place which mattered the most...

I was growing up in a completely dysfunctional family, my brother wasn't doing well then and I got exposed to human insanity and dark energies at a very young age (7yrs), It very weirdly creeped up in our life as if there were negative energies in our new house or in that piece of land from always or it was in some of us that was rapidly gaining strength now. Not just me, but all of us struggled to find peace at home because there was a constant energy of fear and anxiety throughout. Even performing regular daily tasks like having dinner together peacefully as a family or having a normal conversation had become impossible. Family time at home started feeling like a punishment, which is why I kept myself at school as much as possible. I dreaded coming home, and would try to numb myself down as soon as I entered home. My parents were always anxious about when the next outburst from my brother would be, when would he get violent suddenly, when would he threaten to harm us or use profanity to get a reaction from us? He was under some deep psychosis. I was too young to fathom anything that was going on, just tried to distract myself with Television, homework, music and went on living every day. My parents resorted to mainstream medicine and local spiritual healers. My mom had faith in the alternate sciences and had big hopes of receiving help. She went to almost every Godman, Astrologer, Palmist, Healer in town. My parents left no stone unturned. As the years passed by, I saw my brother crawl through his teenage years, his issues only getting more confusing and dangerous with the young reckless energy. Till then he had slapped a faculty at IIM, tried to throw a laborer in the campus from the 1st floor, called the cops over in the hostel campus many times as a threat to scare his fellow roommates, self harmed, punched people at home, ran away from home many times and many other even dark events kept occurring which I don't feel like mentioning. He was under regular psychiatric medication, which would calm his nerves down and allow him to think straight when taken, but was only a temporary solution. It never cured him from inside, because this disorder wasn't on the surface. It was deeper than that and it didn't belong only to him. It felt like we were all destined to suffer with him; it was a part of our soul journey, part of our lessons, some judgement call, some huge pending *karma* and we were facing it for a reason. We had accepted it as our fate and kept dragging our life with it. Over the years, I saw my brother going through the various stages of his condition, from self isolation to verbal abuse, then physical violence and damaging property, and then extreme entitlement and delusion. He was creating stories in his head which he believed were true. He would proudly go about telling everyone his detective stories, of how he solved complicated criminal cases and saved people. Stories of how he was going to receive honorary degrees from his institute and how he was the chief advisor of the current ruling government. He would get more dramatic and aggressive with his delusional story telling when we had any guests over and those would be very anxious moments for us because we wouldn't know how to clean up the mess once he left or to provide any justification to anyone. And then followed the stages where he got into certain addictions and a bit suicidal. He was never the same though; he kept changing every year, kept transforming into something else every time I saw him. He was treated at de addiction centers and kept at some of the best medical facilities in the country. His hygiene levels were very low, with no morals or consciousness. The negative energy I spoke about earlier just didn't leave, sort of. It was following him and following us.

ATTACHMENT TO WHAT THINGS COULD HAVE BEEN AND UNABLE TO LET GO

THE 'TROPHY BOY'

Apart from his condition, before he got wrapped up in his sickness, until 14 yrs of age, he was a very bright and charming boy, very talkative, great at social gatherings, the head boy of his school, always the topper, doing debates, winning quiz competitions, playing cricket, very handsome looking and had a great sense of humor. He could write poems, rhyme while talking (sort of like rapping), was very creative, popular with girls, could charm anyone with his wits and had a good singing voice too. He also was much ahead of his peers, knowing what he wants, what he was going to become in the next 5 years and knew how to get there. He looked very sorted and figured out for all the elders in the family, in the community, family friends and my parents' colleagues, as he was checking all the boxes of the matrix. Overall, he was the trophy boy in the family whom my parents very proudly showed off at any event or social get together. My parents really had big hopes of him doing very well in life, of him making them proud one day. But who knew what was lying ahead of us? Life took a very different turn and literally turned our worlds upside down. It was this perfect boy vision of my parents that they couldn't give up on. They wondered how could their beautiful creation, who was nothing short of a prince, turn into a psychotic patient. Their trophy was breaking right in front of their eyes, their dreams were crumbling and they were getting desperate, trying to fix him. It was the inability to move on from that image they had in mind of his; it was the attachment to that version of their son, who was so perfect, that kept hurting them for decades. They were not able to accept the truth, see the reality for what it is now and not for what it could have been. They kept this hurt, this pain very close to their heart, and it turned them into bitter people. Their entire life now revolved around him, his condition, and his treatments. They forgot to notice there were other members in the family and other events, achievements of others, which could have been a happy moment, which could be celebrated. There was no life, it was sucked out from our environment, anything fun was not allowed, no weekends, no birthdays, new year celebrations or outings. Basically, what I have learned is that whatever you focus on, your energy goes there and that particular thing starts building, your life becomes that. And my family kept focusing on the negative energy, the pain, the trauma way too much and it kept building to a point where they felt lost, cursed, stuck and delusional. If we had known this earlier, we would have only focused on creating happiness, joyful events, and feeling positive energy. It was some kind of generational curse, a pattern, a huge life lesson which we took a very long time to learn.

GROWING UP WITH A KARMIC FAMILY

A Mentally and Emotionally Unstable Mother (Full Blown Narcissist)

A Brother with multiple mental disorders since childhood

A Father who tried standing up to the traumatic patterns but ultimately got sucked into the curse and gave in

Growing up, I dealt with a lot of mommy issues. Dad, being my rock, was always positive, strong and always thought of expanding himself and us in the most positive ways. It was he who kept us going. It was a very tough task for him to handle so many complexities within his family, manage the stress and yet perform incredibly well at his demanding job. My dad is a scientist and maybe because of his background and his nature, he approached every problem with a solution, with a cure, with rationality and compassion for everyone, hearing what everyone has to say and never judging or belittling anyone. Mom, on the other hand became like a competitive older sister. She obsessively wanted to control everyone around her, from the house helps, her kids, people she dealt with at work and even Dad. Extreme unhealthy competition and humiliating anybody who came in with a different opinion, she wouldn't stand any female around her unless she appeared submissive and bowed down to her. She saw everyone as competition or beneath her. The word 'forgiveness' wasn't there in her dictionary. It was in her nature to curse repeatedly, speak ill of her own children's future, and she physically abused anyone she thought she could get away with, who basically wouldn't hit her back. As a child I faced a lot of public humiliation at parties, events, around shopkeepers etc for barely doing anything, for maybe merely expressing what I want. I was discouraged, mocked and interrupted at any given moment by my own mother. I was told I didn't look pretty, that I was dark-skinned which is why I was forbidden to wear certain colors, that even my laugh didn't sound good, it was as if she just didn't want me to bloom, she didn't want me to rise above her, to have my own opinions or to even develop confidence. Deep negative brainwashing and conditioning was taking place at that time. She was threatened by my energy, my talents that I displayed, the attention or compliments I received from others, the fact which I didn't understand until very late. Because we had only heard stories of step mothers being evil from Cinderella days, no one would ever think that your own mother who gave birth to you could also be equally evil.

She would get disturbed and triggered by the tiniest issue in the kitchen or keep brooding on a comment she received weeks ago. We at home would be at the receiving end of her triggers, her wrath. And with my brother's situation getting worse by the day, she was never at peace and never let anybody else be at peace. It was double trouble at home with Brother and Mom losing their mind all the time. Things got very toxic to a point where we were at danger of losing our lives sometimes. One day out of frustration she poured fuel on her and tried to light her up into flames. But that attempt was unsuccessful. She survived as the matches were soaked in oil. It was like she wanted blood on her hands. At times she would do things that had no explanation even from her own side. She behaved like a child who didn't get enough time to live her childhood or was highly cursed and traumatized by something.

These are a few short anecdotes that I am sharing from my childhood which sort of stayed with me for a long time and I had to heal myself a great deal from. I had to understand my mothers mind to forgive her and the whole situation. Some are examples of the generational patterns that my mother and my aunts were trying to pass down to us and my cousins, mostly the daughters. These patterns ran in the bloodline, they all spoke and acted in the same toxic way. Some were very unhealed personal reactions to the negative energy they were experiencing. They were subconscious reactions and also fully aware decisions made in broad daylight when intense pain was being inflicted on me which were even physically injurious and life threatening at times. What they were passing onto us was right according to them which is why they pushed it with utter conviction and stood by it strongly when questioned.

ANECDOTE NO 1: BREAKING PATTERNS OF GENDER INEQUALITY IN THE HOUSEHOLD

I was in the 5th or 6th standard, about 10 yrs old, and we had some guests over for lunch. They were family friends, a mix of uncles, aunties and their children. All the women in our house, my mother, a couple of cousins who were living with us briefly and a kitchen help lady were busy since morning that day and they worked hard to prepare a great 6 course meal with sheer pride. Finally the time came to have lunch together, all the fancy plates, bowls and spoons were lined up on the table, all the guests and the men from our family, which is my Dad and brother, were asked to sit on the dining table. I was wondering which is my seat, where is my plate and why isn't anyone asking me to grab a plate. I asked my mom eagerly about my lunch as I was hungry too and the smell of the amazing food was very appetizing. That is when to my exquisite surprise my mom asked me to not eat with the guests on the dining table, although there was a free chair around the dining table and even if there was none I could have always borrowed a chair and sat at the table. **She said I could eat with the women in the kitchen now or wait for the guests to get up and then eat later at the table.** I was quite shocked because this hadn't happened earlier and I was wondering why I was made to feel this way. I saw the women in the kitchen, some were having their lunch, some waiting to serve the guests and my mom supervising them but not eating anything. It was that ancestral pattern where the women folk would eat at the end, even after toiling in the kitchen so hard since morning, after preparing amazing food all day they would still starve themselves and not reward themselves by enjoying that great food along with the guests. A lot of times some of the courses would even get over by the time everyone ate, and they won't even get a chance to taste those specialties. I never liked this and didn't understand why they had to do this. I would advise them to keep some for them in the kitchen and give away the rest, in that way at least they would have tasted everything they made. I wished the other women in the household would step up and look at themselves differently, as more deserving, as more curious and questioning. At least deserving of making their own decisions of when, what and where to eat, what to wear and when to speak. Around that time my mother had started doing weird things like deciding how much of a second serving I should take while eating at someone's wedding and even went to the extent of giving her measurements for my dress while getting it stitched at a tailor's shop, which I had to start standing up to gradually..

I saw them doing these things but I never let that get to me ever in the past, but that day this pattern tried to engulf me too and I was moderately angry. It's surprising because I was just 10, and even at that age I had a great sense of self respect. I just wasn't going to let myself fall in that trap. There was this ancestral spirit within me which wouldn't let me go through the same patterns. Although I didn't even understand that it was a pattern then, I would normally just follow instructions at home, but when something was genuinely not right, a sense of anger, resentment and deep pain would rise in my blood. I never understood where that came from, but I do now. It was my ancestral connection, my ancestors emoting through me, living through me, and not letting injustice happen again through me. I immediately stood up for myself saying I was not going to eat in the kitchen with them, I wanted my seat and plate to be set up on the dining table and I was only going to have my lunch there. My mother wasn't very startled because by then she was used to seeing me get my way when I demanded certain things. I was quiet and polite but there was a sense of power in my silence, because when I broke my silence and demanded something everyone knew I was doing that for a reason and I couldn't be denied then. I was given what I wanted when I spoke with that innate power and a sense of self even when I was in my pre teens.

ANECDOTE NO 2: NOT REACTING TO REGULAR ATTEMPTS AT BREAKING MY SELF CONFIDENCE

As I said earlier I was a quiet, innocent child who barely had a voice and I was taken advantage because of that. I remember that day very well, I was barely 10 yrs old and there were guests about to arrive at home. I was about to get ready and my mother as usual came over with the mood to humiliate me and says, **'Better wear some good clothes, or they will think you are the maid of the house'.** I know a lot of you would be thinking how could a mother say this to her own daughter who is so young. What kind of parenting is this? And how could I live with these people? This is an example of what exactly a mother or any parent should not be saying to their children. But I am letting you know this is the exact recipe of how you break a child's confidence bit by bit everyday. When you say something like that to a 10 year old, you are preparing that child to become a monster later. They can become very bitter and low in confidence in their adolescence and never expect anything good from the world. Their faith in goodness starts shattering, they see the world with the eyes of condemnation and want to punish everybody around them later when they receive a position of authority in society. That day, I was supposed to feel upset or angry right? after what happened but very surprisingly I didn't even feel a thing, never argued or said anything back. I had realized this only much later that there was something protecting me in those situations. Like you know I was spiritually protected since birth, it never allowed the hurt to penetrate deep. I was going through these dark events almost every other day but somehow these harsh comments wouldn't hit me as hard as they were intended. I would be kind of numb at home anyway and these harsh energies would just slide down my back like water dripping down a duck's back. It didn't break me, I never felt the need to react and argue back, as if I knew saying anything would be very pointless at that time. It would only make my mom excited enough to throw more harsh words at me or not serve me dinner that night and at the end I won't win because I was still a kid, sort of powerless living in my parents house under them.

ANECDOTE NO 3: NOT REACTING TO SUDDEN ATTEMPTS OF SEVERE PHYSICAL INJURY/LIFE THREATS

My parents had moved to Delhi around 2005 - 2010. I was doing my undergraduate in Design at NIFT, Bangalore, then and would visit my parents during semester breaks. I hated going home during the holidays. Since I left home after 12th, I barely went back. I never missed home. It was the opposite of homesickness. I would make excuses to stay back in the campus and hangout, do part-time jobs, work backstage at fashion shows or as a hostess at various other events, earn some pocket money and stay in my own zone far away from anything that reminded me of chaos. But at times the narcissistic parent would need her scapegoat to blame things on. You can read about this dynamic online also because it is very relevant to the Chosen Ones. You will find a lot of information. My family would insist on seeing me during my semester breaks, and with a lot of reluctance, I would sometimes book the tickets and visit them. Only to realise that they had called me to ruin my holidays, I wouldn't know it was deliberate back then, I would even complain to them about my holidays getting wasted with family drama and no fun, but of course my words were falling on deaf ears, they would brush it off immediately and discourage me to bring it up again. How could they create fun for me when they had never seen it? Their answers and body language were trying to tell me that they were going through huge issues with my brother's sickness and that was the only thing all of us needed to focus on. How could I think about myself, ask for anything fun while something so grievous was taking place in the household? Right?

During one of these dreaded holidays, I had been to Delhi when my dad had taken an emergency transfer just so that he could be with the family and look after them. It was the winter, and I was there for two weeks, which felt so long because I was dying to come back to the campus hostel. The whole household still felt so cursed and troubled. Mom was never feeling good about anything and my bro was getting out of control. One evening me and my mother went out to get some groceries, the shopping was all done, and we were waiting to cross the road. I was pretty nonchalant, looking at my phone and casually staring at the vehicles on the road. At that moment, something crazy happened and even to this date, I have not confronted my mother about it. **She pushed me from the back while a bus was coming from the side. She literally pushed me under a bus with the intention to kill me or hurt me physically in a critical way.** I was strong, so I held myself back; the bus didn't touch me and nothing happened; I turned back to ask what was that, but my mom acted like it was nothing. It was a failed attempt to throw me under a bus, but because it didn't materialize; she had disappointment on her face and without any questions or further understanding we headed back home. My mother, being a full-blown narcissist, played her ways of not taking any accountability of her actions. She downplayed the whole incident and literally acted like nothing happened. We reached home, and I told my dad about how she pushed me in front of a bus. My Dad was shocked too, but he also couldn't ask her anything directly. She was standing right there; she heard everything but did not utter a single word; **it was as if we all had accepted that it was the doing of a highly mentally and emotionally unstable person who has no control of her own emotions or actions, who is way too troubled to judge right from wrong.** We were just happy that I wasn't hurt in any way and was back home safe. Spirit had my back. I wasn't going to get hurt, but I realized that day it wasn't safe to be with her alone at home or outdoors. Now, when I recall those moments, it feels like a lifetime ago. This incident still triggers me somewhat out of all the stories, but I calm myself down because I no longer want to create any bad karma cycles with these people. I have grown and healed so much from that time. But I feel the same sadness, the same helplessness for her, who was so stuck and under such negative influence, negative entities had her entirely in their control, but I don't feel the bitterness as much because it's been so long and I have really worked hard on my shadows for years to forgiven them. We can't brush these incidents off our shoulders thinking at least I came out without a scratch safe because **they still are very grave and evil.** I Thank God as none of her attempts were successful, but that doesn't make my life experience any easier.

ANECDOTE NO 4: FILED A FALSE POLICE COMPLAINT AGAINST ME FOR PHYSICAL ABUSE

There have been way too many incidents in between these years but for the fourth story I am fast forwarding to the year 2023, this incident which was the final nail in the coffin, which severed the cords very abruptly and transformed me further into developing my own support system even more strongly. This was the time when I was writing this book in 2023, I had moved in with my parents to their new flat, thinking things had changed over so many years, thinking my mother was more civil now as she had turned to Christianity looking for answers that she never found her entire lifetime. They were growing old and tired of taking care of my brother. They wanted my presence and assistance at that time, but at the same time they had other negative agendas in their mind of trapping and using me for their benefit. They were not ready to give me any credit for what I had achieved in my own life living by myself all these years, downplaying my growth in career & business. Me on the other hand was unaware of all this. I wanted to help, support and reunite the family, which I thought was required at that time. My lifestyle was very different from my family. My lifestyle choices, beliefs and self love were at another level. Due to the healing and inner work put in through so many years, I had changed immensely. I was reflecting health, light, beauty, and peace. I was happy with what I was earning and was working very hard to reach my goals. My mother was highly envious of what she saw in me. She saw my confidence reaching new heights, which she had tried to kill since childhood. She saw my spiritual rank elevate to a different degree and my authority rise above her at times and she wasn't able to believe it. This was the first time my parents were witnessing me after I had begun my healing journey. They barely kept in touch with me afterall. It was utterly shocking and horrific for her. Although my parents were well off, they were stuck in the lack mindset, poverty mindset, which didn't let them enjoy life. Now, out of sheer jealousy and shock, she kept sending me evileye. It was very easy now because we were under the same roof. She was hoping for my downfall, trying to mistreat me like before, frisking my room in my absence and strongly opposed if I practised any of my regular spiritual rituals. I started having hair fall, some skin issues etc, but I was being very productive still. I had started looking for a new place for myself because I knew I wouldn't be able to stay with them for long. They haven't changed at all for my information and have crushed high hopes; they were still the same, just pretending to look calm and religious to the Church they went to and the outside world. One evening, I remember it being a super full moon, my mother was trying to trigger me into a fight all evening. I kept ignoring her like usual. I felt like something had gotten into her that evening. Her general negative tendencies were heightened by the full moon and she wanted to piss me off and transfer some negative energy to me so that she could feel at peace. At dinner time again she kept asking unnecessary questions about my profession, my monthly profit, about how I am wasting my education by choosing to not work in that field, how I haven't been able to prove my talent to the world and to them, etc. She kept picking these things on purpose because she knew how serious I was with my work. She could see how hard I was working every day. She knew she could trigger me by insulting my work. I kept ignoring it for a long time, but I guess even I got carried away with the intensity of the full moon that night. I decided to show her who I am now, no longer that 10 yr old child who got bullied until she burst into tears. There was a lot of arguing. I even pulled out stories, and it got very ugly. I brought out all the stuff which Dad had told me during his frustrated moments, how she physically abused the maids, misbehaved with her daughter-in-law, even falsely accused my 75 yr old dad of having an affair with the maid and how she has been getting demonic attacks at night, etc. She wasn't aware that I knew everything; I knew it all, but let her act as a church going God fearing innocent pious woman. She was shocked once I opened the entire bag of sins in front of her and now that she needed to hide again; she had to blame it all on dad. I had to drag her out as she began cursing the temple in my room, blaming it on my gods, my rituals, and spirituality. The whole fight went on for hours. I had locked my door, but the yelling was continuous. I didn't tear up at all during this fight as if a voice from within spoke up, **'This is not the time to cry, you have cried enough, this is the time to fight back'. So I did. With all my power, I did not show mercy.**

The next morning, as usual, I woke up to finish some regular recordings and video editing. I wasn't feeling a thing; I put everything that happened at night behind me; I was just worried about finishing deadlines. I could see my mother going nuts in the house, though. She couldn't digest what she went through. She had decided she was going to make a big deal for everyone out of it. She was already calling up people, fighting, complaining, threatening to leave home, etc. **As I was finishing my work, I got a call from the nearby police station that my mom had filed a police complaint against me for domestic abuse.** This is what Narcissists do: they trigger others very hard to get a reaction and then finally, when they get it; they play a victim for the fight they only started and then take legal help against you to make you look bad. I managed the situation calmly, never had to visit the station, started locking my room everytime I stepped out and had decided to move out asap without giving them any notice. But karma hit my mom hard that very same day. She was hospitalized, unable to breathe, had major complications, and had to be kept in the ICU for several days. I intuitively was told that her voice would be taken away if she kept bad-mouthing me further and worse. Her life might get cut short if she continued to trouble me from here on. When she was back from the hospital, I got the proof of what I intuitively heard. Her voice was literally gone. She wasn't able to speak; it was a squeaking mouse like sound that was coming from here. I told my dad this was her karma for hurting everyone and asked them to not come in my way anymore. I avoided them at all costs, making my arrangements to move out, and swore I would never let myself get into any kind of situation like this. Thankfully, my ancestors, spirit guides and the divine had taken control of the whole situation. They protected me fiercely and made sure I was unharmed. My ancestors spoke through me very loud for hours at night and at 5am sometimes, it was a man's voice that came out through me, very loud, angry and curseful. I was channeling my Ancestors. They were furious with my parents and this whole situation. They cursed my parents for attacking a divine child. The whole building could hear it. Yes, such incidents did take place. I witnessed my male ancestors speaking out prophetic words very loud through me.

Dad, on the other hand was still very scared. He was a victim of domestic abuse, constant threats, emotional and psychological abuse. I could see it in his behavior every day. Always panicking, over-explaining, making decisions in anxiety, taking on more household work than required just to keep himself busy and out of sight, walking on eggshells, not knowing when to stand up, whose side to take even when he knows who's at fault. He was going through a lot, but he wasn't ready to change anything either. Everytime I nudged him to speak up, he would say he is too old and tired for that. It's his time to leave earth. He would not achieve anything by standing up at this point. It would only lead to more fights and stress. He just wanted to leave Earth without any regrets or conflicts. He did love my mom still very unconditionally, in spite of what she had been up to. He saw that vulnerable, hurt and withered lady within who was just completely broken, very unhappy. Who couldn't see any of her dreams being fulfilled, who didn't have anything to celebrate, she had everything but still so ungrateful, to God and those around her, she had given up her entire life to darkness and kept running recklessly to fix her son. He knew she would be nothing without him; she was alive and breathing just because my dad was her supply. That is what narcissists do, they always need a human supply from whom they feed positive energy daily because they have none of their own, without whom they cannot live, not in a good and romantic way, but in a very dark toxic and dangerous way, whom they also ridicule, keep small, keep on a leash rather so they won't leave them. My dad was that being who she kept on a leash, fed from every day and mocked endlessly, making him feel worthless. My dad knew all of it, he was so used to it, that is what he called a 'Happy Marriage' lol, because he hadn't seen anything else, not felt anything better. Having a full-blown, psychotic, narcissistic spouse for 45yrs who you still love it has to be something. You definitely need some divine powers to be able to do that. Most of the Indian couples we know who have lived for 30+ years together turn into something like this, they keep living and dying at the same time in this dynamic, which they all call a secure life, a happily married life, which they promote and try to sell to all their children. Only if they knew what was beyond it, only if they could take a break and experience something else for a couple of years, they would maybe never go back to it. I don't know what to feel about them. Pity yes and a lot of mixed emotions. So basically my dad had made up his mind and I couldn't bring him to change anything. To what I told him in a very practical way is that I was still very young and had many years to live, many things to do, which is why I don't keep any liabilities like him. I was free to do whatever I want, go wherever I want and that won't change, I wouldn't let family issues or any drama get to me, I won't change my opinions and lifestyle even if I have to cut them off or keep them at a distance. I made it very clear to them that none of them would be allowed around me or in my future, of course no one liked it, even the distant relatives wondered what was so grave this time, some of them knew only one side of the story, they all are part of the old system after all who would only ask you to fall back and be part of the system but I guess this event was definitely the last nail in the coffin.

THE DISTANT RELATIVES ALL CAME OVER WITH THE SAME SYMPTOMS AND ISSUES.

These are the extended family members from my mother's side, essentially. My mother was the 9th child, the last one, youngest one out of 10 or 11 kids. A couple of the siblings did not survive and died in their early childhood, but 9 survived. And each of these siblings of hers have 3 to 4 kids each, so it becomes a huge family of uncles, aunts and 1st cousins alone. From an early age, I noticed each of these families have at least one person who's suffering from a psychological disorder, either the child, the mother or the father, at least one person in each unit is mentally distressed and sometimes more than one.

The families who are identified with generational curses or heavy toxic patterns can have these curses in different kinds. Sometimes there will be curses of poverty, people unable to go beyond a certain income bracket or remaining under a line even after many generations, in some cases there will be curses of some kind of addictions, people having disturbed and ill-functioning families because of heavy addiction multiple substances where they are not able to see each other as family even, in some cases it will be a curse of death, family members dying prematurely and not crossing a certain age limit, it can also be a gender related curse where only the men are dying, not a single man is surviving in the family, where not just the sons but even the son in laws who are entering the family through marriage are falling prey to the curse.

Now in my mothers bloodline there was this curse of mental illness and it was there in every family, either the aunts, uncles or at least one child was going through some kind of major disturbance to a point where they had to take medicines and clinical advice. And because of that one person, each individual family unit was getting wrecked layer by layer over the years. The medical industry has given all kinds of names to the symptoms of these ongoing generational curses as conditions and disorders, but a lot of times even they are unable to diagnose certain strange behavior. They justify them with certain imbalances of chemicals in the brain, coping mechanisms, severe social anxiety and under developed or over developed nerve sections in parts of the brain, etc. We had interacted with numerous specialists all over the country for my brother and other people in the family, so gradually after a point, after decades we could predict what the doctors would say. We understood their diagnosis and treatment patterns. We even got disappointed many times when the prescribed medicine wouldn't be able to give anything more than a temporary solution, even after promising many things. That is when we had to turn to alternate healing sciences and spirituality. But we know what we have seen, we understand the medical aspect of it, the deficiencies in the physical body yes, but these deformities and deficiencies are being caused by the age old bloodline patterns and curses. The trauma and curses run in the blood.

These are curses for real and I had started observing all these things very early. I was Barely 10 years old. My family unit was the one living in the city, in the capital city of the state. We had access to the best doctors, hospitals and other specialists. So a lot of my extended family would travel down to our city from the villages and other towns and stay at our place while they were visiting doctors and getting their treatments done.

That is when it became more and more obvious to me. They would all come with the same symptoms, complain of the same discomfort, similar treatments and then the same recurring symptoms which won't go away. People becoming violent, cursing, looking at everyone around with suspicion, unable to control their emotions, getting visions, hallucinations, nightmares, skipping their medicines, running away from home, feeling deep pain in certain parts of their body, feeling suicidal, etc.

It was so obvious what was going on, but no one was doing the calculations, no one was connecting the dots. Some were feeling better seeing the others in stress, knowing that they were not the only ones holding the trauma, but no one was talking about it. Deep down in their subconscious, people knew it, but they didn't want to believe it and bring it to the surface. They were thinking, 'what's the point of bringing the past back? It's too much work to dig up stuff that they barely are sure of, and who had that kind of time and intention in the first place'. It was that kind of thing going on, but only a fool would not notice. It was like 'that' obviously. I started connecting the dots back then itself and I used to write essays on these findings for school and college projects sometimes. I felt like I had just scratched the surface and there was so much more to dig deep and learn about. It can't be all a coincidence and I was quite perplexed as I got into the depths. When you see it happening in each and every family, like at least 10 to 15 families, which is no joke, you know it has been trickling down from centuries.

BIRTH OF THE CHOSEN ONE

Toxic patterns of how the elders mistreated each other, their children or their slaves. They were very entitled to it, very nonchalant about passing down the dark venomous patterns to the next generation, without ever giving even a moment to understand what they were doing was right or wrong. They were living within the set rules and assumed that 'this happens here, this is what has been going on since so many hundreds of years, and this is how it will be, it's not going to change, who are we to change and why should we change anything, when we have experienced a certain pattern all our life you must experience the same too, as it comes under the family traditions, whether wrong or right'. That was the norm, that was the mindset they carried and they were very casual about it.

It was going on for so long and then finally in that family one child had to be born who was the reason for everything to end, all of that to end and very surprisingly, very divinely orchestrated that this whole thing is, that child had to be **me**, who had to understand everything from a very young age. Grasp all the signs, symptoms and connect all the dots, do thorough research, analyze everything and go through the precautionary measures to protect herself and future generations from knowing the future prediction and patterns.

Of course, once people saw I was showing the signs of somebody like that there was a lot of opposition. Opposition not just from humans but from the enemy, the collective universal negative energy. The collective negative energy which does not want a Chosen One to do its job, to perform what they are exactly born for, they don't want a Chosen One to fulfil their purpose. And that negative energy which we call the enemy keeps manifesting in different people as opposition, whether that is a member of family, friends, colleagues, lovers, partners, potential partners and even landlords sometimes. Random landlords whose houses you are living in and even complete strangers on the road walking past you trying to trigger you so bad. It started manifesting everywhere and was trying to constantly stop me from doing my thing. Family being the closest entities are capable of hurting you the most, which is why they definitely manifest through narcissistic family members. My family recognized me as the truth teller. They were very scared that the truth teller was now going to expose everything, disclose all their actions done in the dark. They wanted to shut me up; they tried many things many times but failed over and over again.

I am the last person in the bloodline, the youngest child of the youngest parent. This is how the pattern shows, even in the other dysfunctional families and their lineages. There will be one last child, the final last child from the youngest lot of siblings, that is mostly the Chosen One from what I have understood, from other people as well who have been talking about this. I wasn't surprised to know that my mother is the youngest out of nine kids and I am her younger daughter. I had to wait till my turn came and had to take my birth as the youngest one. So I am that person who has been chosen for this task. Most of the time, the youngest one is Chosen because with that there is the best possibility to start a completely healed and renewed bloodline for the dynasty. The youngest one will be able to start a fresh line of healed lineage with a different positive set of upbringing and parenting patterns which will integrate with the future leaving the troubled patterns of older siblings and their children far behind where it cannot influence them anymore.

If I decide, the bloodline can end with me. But if I decide to take the lineage ahead, take the bloodline ahead then I must heal every part of me, parts that cannot be seen, those dark broken unhealed toxic shadowy parts of me in the unknown spiritual world which even I am not completely aware of, which I try to hide at times or dont believe exist but come out when I get too comfortable. Once I heal all of those hidden broken soul fragments, integrate them and only then I take the generation forward. The toxic cycles end with me, the entire curse breaks here with me, they end here with me and I decide if I want to take the lineage forward or not after deep healing everything. So it's a huge responsibility on my shoulders and on a lot of other Chosen One's shoulders. I know that most of the trauma I have been able to heal through several years with a lot of dedication, a lot of understanding and patience. I have been able to break but some stuff is still there. It doesn't end so easily, it requires continuous effort of years, constant revisiting, rechecking if anything new has resurfaced, if there are any new triggers and immediately take that into notice and start the healing work for it again.

We must know that every trigger that surfaces is only a sign to identify what caused that trigger and work on that broken part immediately. I'm tackling the big ones at the moment, the biggest of the curses I have dealt with, they are slowly moving away with my work but there is more stuff to be done. Everytime I thought I was done, another broken part would resurface and trigger me. I am so grateful for these triggers for they are our teachers.

CHAPTER 4

PECULIARITIES AND PRIVILEGES OF THE CHOSEN ONES

If you have been able to read the previous chapters successfully and come till this page of this book, then I know you are relating yourself as a Chosen. You are maybe in tears getting reminded of your own childhood, your own stories and have this deep hunger to know more. You have understood one thing for sure, is that no matter how many times you hit rock bottom, however dark your days had been, no matter the number of long stormy nights you went through and even if the most devilish person was sent to attack you, you were not harmed. In spite of all the darkness sent your way you were unharmed, you came out of it without a scratch. You were given a huge amount of strength and resilience every time you needed it. And everytime you passed a difficult test with your own calibre you were promoted and sent to the next stage, the next level to receive the next set of lessons along with the next set of tasks. In this way you gathered a lot of character, strength and spiritual authority. You kept getting promoted each time you followed through which slowly gained you higher ranks.

These are spiritual ranks of the spiritual realm. And along with these ranks come a lot of perks, such as spiritual authority and spiritual protection.

SPIRITUAL AUTHORITY AND DIVINE 'Z' CLASS PROTECTION

You know why you were Chosen? Because you are the most powerful and capable candidate of the entire generation, the previous generation and the previous generation in your bloodline. It's not an easy task. It's hell of a big mission. And it's not everyone's cup of tea. No one was going to be able to do it unless it was you. People don't even know what kind of struggles you've gone through. If you tell them, they won't even believe it. And if some of those people in your family, even from your own generation, were put in those kinds of dangerous circumstances, they won't be alive today. But you have survived. Now you know what kind of power you hold. The differences that you have because of which you were mistreated, you were singled out. Those are the exact things which make you very, very unique. And if you work on them and expand them, they can become your superpowers. And that is the exact reason they made you not believe in yourself. Those exact things were used against you. They tried real hard to dim those exact gifts because those are your powers. And if you come to know about your own superpowers, you become too powerful for anybody. Then nobody can hold you down. They can't do anything to you. That was the holding back strategy that was used since your childhood, not just now. It's the devil's work, they do that. You're going to come to know a lot more about yourself, about how, why, when, where and what is instored for you in this lifetime. A lot of things about your purpose, about how you're going to do everything will be revealed to you in time as you get ready. This is just a small initiation, coming across this book is also a part of your initiation. This is just the beginning! But from here on, your path is glorious. And you are going to take full reins, you're going to take complete charge and do what you are supposed to do. You're going to answer your soul's call, your heart's call which is desperately calling you out. Get to know about your ancestors a little more, who they were, what kind of work they did. You'll get to know more stuff about it slowly through those connections by observing the patterns that are there in your bloodline. Things that are still coming up in you, things that trigger you, things that trigger your parents. All those are traumas. Think about your childhood. Observe the times as they went by, observe what kept coming again and again, which needed your attention back then and which needs your attention now. But be very happy, be very grateful for having this life, for being reincarnated as a Chosen One. Your soul has that power. Your soul has chosen this life and you must honor it. You are being called to have this explosive, dynamite kind of life. Everybody doesn't get to live it like that. A lot of people have very mundane lives, very dull lives, which go on in the 3D without them ever discovering themselves or even attempting to learn about the reason for their existence. But your life isn't going to be like that. Thank your ancestors, thank your angels for having protected you all this while. In spite of all the obstacles and darkness you still are standing on your two feet. You're still safe and alive. That has happened due to their grace, your ancestors have been watching you because you're the Chosen One. A chosen one has a lot of security. It's like the 'Z level security' which the politicians get. You have 'Z class spiritual security' around you all the time because you're a Chosen one. They are doing a lot behind the veil so be very grateful for everything they are doing for you. These are huge privileges. So have faith and thank them for doing this.

You might have come across times when you are casually doing your thing at a supermarket or you are just walking down the street browsing your phone and strangers try to approach you for a conversation. Not to sell you anything but they get awfully drawn to you and they smile a lot for a stranger, or just stare at you, unable to look away. Or when you are meeting up with someone for work, post the work talk they kind of get very comfortable with you and start sharing their personal information. They might even discuss their personal issues and expect some form of consultation from you. They feel a strange magnetic pull towards you which makes them trust you with their secrets and personal information. At a very subconscious level they feel you've got an answer to their questions, they think you might be able to do something for them. This is a sign of having Spiritual authority, the intuitive vibe of something else walking with you, of a higher power being by your side. And because you are an empath you will most of the time end up listening to them and giving a portion of your time and guidance to them.

Maybe you are sitting there reading your book in the park or an open air small cafe and people might just come and sit next to you or opposite to you out of the blue. People want to generally connect with individuals who have a certain amount of power or authority even if they don't say it out loud. It's a part of human behavior and the need for safety, security as a survival instinct, which is why they act silly around Chosen spiritual individuals. Sometimes they themselves don't know why they are acting that way, because a lot of these behaviors get triggered subconsciously when they sense your innate soul power and wisdom and get inquisitive the more they witness you. But as a Chosen One even without you having a powerful or influential profession or position and a massive 3D identity, people will naturally come and hover around you because the Spiritual Authority and High rank surpasses any form of 3D Identity or character that we are playing in the matrix.

You also might witness these kind of events at a gathering where people deny you your rights, like right to speech, whereby let's say there was an issue and a question was asked, you raise your hand, you had the answer, they have seen you but they refuse to give you the microphone, they don't want to give you a chance. Or even in a family meeting they are finding a solution to a specific problem and for some reason everybody else could speak apart from you, they never wanted you to speak. Now when something like this happens to you, you understand that there are very low vibrational people sitting in this meeting and very subconsciously they feel like there's something you have got to say which is very powerful and whatever it is that you are going to say will outshine them, although they could be complete strangers and distant family members who don't know much about you. People realize you have got an otherworldly authority and they don't want you to speak because when you speak you may sometimes utter massive truths which they have been covering for a long time, lies that they have been spreading for decades. This shows that you have Spiritual authority.

Spiritual protection also is about receiving insights about things that have happened in the past and are going to occur in the future, which you can protect yourself from. Examples could be receiving divine guidance about taking certain turns on your way to work so that you can avoid delays, missing your daily bus to avoid an accident and premonitions of future events to steer clear from any form of damage.

3 REASONS YOU ARE HIGHLY FAVORED AND PROTECTED

One thing that people don't understand is why are Chosen people so highly protected and favored. They are protected for a reason, they are surrounded by an army of spiritual bodyguards, it's a huge army that watches over them at all times, even in their sleep, in their dream state and also during their intimate moments. Even when I spoke about the great entities protecting me all the time, many have wondered what is the need for such protection. They are basically completely unaware of the lifestyle that a Chosen one has.

• TURBULENT EVENTS ALL THROUGHOUT THEIR LIFE

The first reason is that The Chosen Ones tend to experience very difficult situations all through their life, being the black sheep originally even their own parents can be afraid of them, they are poisoned by their partners in relationships and experience heavy envy from their siblings, co-workers and close friends. These connections try to damage you physically, mentally, socially and spiritually, in whichever way they can, by speaking ill on your name, your life, attacking your reputation, your character and trying to change your destiny through that.

Inexplicable and dangerous events take place on their journey but you will wonder and ask yourself this question, How come you are still here, how are you still alive? And I am here to tell you that the reason why you have survived everything and you're still here is because you're being protected by divine entities all the time, there are forces behind you that you do not see with your naked eyes. The universe has chosen you for a reason, but it does not mean that the Chosen One's journey is always going to be smooth and problem free.

You will see obstacles over and over again but you will have this inner knowing that you're gonna make it through the next day. Chosen Ones may have false FIRs, people trying to sue them without a reason. They might have been in some near-death experiences, might be abandoned by the whole world and even lived in shelters like an orphan while their family was alive. There are many of these drastic low points in life, extreme critical situations that they had to deal with but behind the scenes God will always give them a second chance. God will give you multiple chances and give you enough guidance so you can follow your intuition and save yourself the next time.

Chosen Ones have been assigned important tasks and missions in their lifetime and they are not allowed to abort the mission, there can be delays but it has to be completed by them. It doesn't matter who tries to do what against you, medical emergencies or calamities, narcissists trying to hunt you down or obsessed psychopaths trying to clone you and wipe you out. We can talk about it all and the list is endless, but the truth is that the universe has got your back and you will fulfill the mission as soon as the dust settles and the sky is clear. Later on when you look back and connect the dots you will see what it was, your mission and how everytime the higher forces tricked everything and everyone else to make you reach your point, your goal. So do not worry about the experiences you're going through at the moment, every difficult circumstance, every delay and rejection is only going to lead you to your next step, the next person, the next opportunity while loading you up with the necessary armor and weaponry.

Every relationship you get into as a Chosen One is according to the divine order. There will be a task, a mission and something that you will need to learn from them or a very important lesson that you will teach them. There will be something that God will want you to see, which is the reason why you will be put in those kinds of connections and relations. You and the person are supposed to go through an experience through which both people will learn a lesson, that not only provides deep knowledge but also prepares you to enter the next level. It can be a karmic connection also, it can be a long term or short term situation where you get triggered big time, then learn to identify the wounds behind the triggers and then heal the hidden trauma, which basically leads you to your authentic self and helps you find yourself.

• THEY ARE TRUE EMPATHS WHO POSSESS A SACRED GOLDEN HEART

The second reason why God has continuously favored a Chosen One is because they are most likely super empaths. If you are carrying out God's mission you will need to empathize with the people around you, put yourself in their shoes and feel their pain so that you can help them. As a Chosen it is in your nature to forgive a lot of people, you're going to have to forgive your narcissistic parents, your abusive partners, all the people you met in your life who caused tremendous harm towards you. Dear Chosen, a lot of people might misread you, thinking your emotions are your weakness, but this empathy of yours is your superpower, which you use to detach and survive. You have been blessed with this compassion because you need it to thrive in life. So if you look at your life as a Chosen One you will also realize that regardless of what you've been through, regardless of the things that have happened to you, you have continuously spread love out there into the universe and you have continuously loved people uncon-ditionally. You have refused to take revenge, you have refused to destroy other people with your own accumulated trauma over the years. You have refused to project that trauma onto other people. You have decided to use your empathy to free yourself each and every time, by detaching yourself from any feelings of anger, rage or revenge. You have come into the state of acceptance that everything happens for a reason, that even these weird and difficult encounters are for a reason and you show them empathy. Once you are able to empathize with your worst enemies you will rise much higher above them, and you will free yourself from those repeated toxic cycles. Empathy has many deep layers to it which can be used strategically for tackling other deep issues. This divine protection from God is to protect your golden heart, which is a rare possession. You will have to understand that this golden heart has to still keep doing its work, it has to keep at its purpose, it can't stop doing its thing. Spreading joy and bright light is its divine purpose in its entire lifetime which will also need divine support. Many energies will keep coming at it to break the golden heart, ruin its glory, bring it to shame so that it doesn't do its job. Hence the divine constantly provides the Chosen with extra protection, extra emotional support so that they can enjoy their empathy, use it to its fullest potential and keep that sacred golden heart of theirs safe.

• THEY ARE ON DIFFICULT ASSIGNMENTS WITH HIGHER RISKS

As a Chosen you are on difficult assignments at various stages of your life, which you cannot avoid or escape. These tasks are designed for you specifically keeping your purpose and destiny in mind so that you get the exact necessary lessons, not just any lessons mind it, these are the predetermined lessons which will help you get closer to your life purpose, which is why they also involve higher risks. Once you complete these assignments you will activate the precise skills required to go forward with the next phase of your mission. And this process follows through in your entire lifetime, over and over again, till you get equipped enough to take on the biggest mission. These assignments often involve karmic connections and soul contracts, people you are in deep relationships with, could be your spouse who you think are in for the long haul but actually has been placed in just to assist you with the assignments. People you work with or even your parents who are actually the original and longest soul contracts. You are unaware of the truth of these people in the beginning, your guards are not up initially, your boundaries are not strong and you trust them, which is why the divine keeps a thorough eye on you and keeps you in a protected bubble. While you carry out these assignments and begin to unfold your lessons there is always a possibility where these karmics try to stop you from going ahead with the tasks and become obstacles in your path. Depending on how important the task is for your growth they will always create struggle and bring in undue stress for you. They can even try bringing in physical, mental, spiritual, social, emotional and even reputational harm to you directly or indirectly through a third party, sometimes they will also try to take you out completely, which can get kind of dark and very serious. But *but but* because you are the Chosen, you will be protected from many such attempts, no harm will be allowed to touch you. And all the negative energy that was being directed at you will be sent back to the senders with interest. Always remember energy does not die or disappear, it merely transforms, changes its form and moves from one state to another. Where do you think all of that energy will go? It cannot disappear into thin air because it couldn't touch you, it will simply go back to the sender, it will do the same thing that it was supposed to in the first place but only multiple folds. Those who tried causing damage in any form will have all of that negative energy backfired on them, they basically would dig their own grave every time they attempt causing harm.

And this whole phenomenon occurs due to the grace and divine protection of the most High.

Nonetheless, sometimes you feel like you are at the receiving end of spiritual and psychic attacks, because that is what your opposition will resort to at the end when nothing else works against you. They will try to attack your name, tarnish your reputation at your workplace and in the family, but they will see that none of that is really working. People still love you, support you, want to be with you because they see the bright white light in your energetic field and you remain unfazed no matter what is thrown in your way. People even defend your name behind your back and ultimately acknowledge the fact that the opposition was simply slandering your name out of envy. In this scenario the opposition gets highly frustrated and looks out for other hidden ways to attack you. In that desperation they resort to energy attacks and psychic attacks, to knock you off your own stable energy, your mental balance and sometimes to syphon your energy for their personal agendas. But because you are a Chosen and you have a deep connection with the divine, you come out of such attacks very fast, even if you feel the heaviness for sometime. The divine lets you experience the episode for a short while at a surface level to build your immunity and shortly after takes you out of it.

WHY ARE CHOSEN ONES UNFAZED BY MAGIC SPELLS & SPIRITUAL ATTACKS

The whole science behind the Spiritual attacks or Black magic is basically about sending negative energy to a person, to throw them off their stable physical, mental or emotional energy. To make them lose their stability which in return causes them to make wrong decisions, miss out on opportunities, create delays and lack of inspiration, lose hope in their work or life and eventually not fulfill their life purpose. Like I have mentioned earlier in this book, our real enemy is only the collective dark energy of the universe which fights with the collective light force of the universe and not humans really. It's a battle of the dark vs the light like always. The collective universal dark energy is what manifests through humans, situations and circumstances to bring us bad luck and ill results. When a person sends negative energy to another we must understand that it is the collective dark forces at work and it has taken that individual in its control. We can send both positive and negative energy to a person right, while healers and lightworkers send you positive white light and healing energy to heal you and make you feel better, to make your life force stronger in the form of prayers and well wishes. Similarly people can also send negative energy in the form of spells, spells of all kinds, spells as minor as getting fired from a job, not getting a promotion to as severe as a death spell, basically removing the entire life force out of you. This is when people think they can play God in your life, they think they can unalive you just by doing some kitchen spells or paying someone to get a dark ritual done along with animal sacrifices etc. People go to very evil extremes when they get consumed by the negative energy. But they forget that life and death and even every little detail of another person's life is in God's hands and not theirs. Other ways of sending negative energy is gossip, ill wishes, speaking misfortune on their life regularly, sending evil eye, giving negative energy to anything that they are consuming, like food or drinks, sucking their life force while they are sitting next to them or talking to them even over the phone like an energy vampire. Trying to steal someone's beauty, their voice, their unique style, way of speaking etc. People also try to syphon your pure bright healing energy and try to use it for their own benefit, and also in the most hopeless way people sometimes try to exchange destiny, they try to conduct some sort of a ceremony or make use of any cosmic portal to swap destinies with another person. It gets sad, desperate and highly stupid to a point where people start believing that these things are possible, under the heavy influence of evil energy and emotions. The negative energy makes these people believe that these things are possible and makes them take action towards such behavior, which ultimately does them harm. Because always remember even when people work for the devil, the negative is not here to reward them, it will only fool them and bring them destruction. The negative energy was only fooling them all this while keeping them in illusions. Whichever evil entity, deity or lower vibration form they were connecting to, speaking to or praying to, taking orders from and guidance from won't be there to save them once karma starts hitting hard. It's highly foolish of anybody who thinks they can beat God or even come close to disobeying God's orders by following lower vibrational entities. These emotions are mostly jealousy, envy, turning into hate because they see lack within themselves, they sort of are unable to see their own unique qualities, their own gifts hold no value to them, they compare themselves with another person, they want to embody the same qualities like another person but are unable to. Which is wrong from the beginning because no matter how good another person is in whichever way, we need to realize that we also have our own God gifted unique talents, which is why there is no need for comparison ever in the first place. Yes, we can get inspired from others and try to improve ourselves but it is clearly maniacal when you are so crazy that you want to swap your destiny with another person. You want to live another person's daily life and out do them without knowing what struggles that person has. If you were even able to swap your destiny you will not just get that person's favors and gifts but also all their life problems, their stress and trauma.

WHAT CAN WE DO TO PROTECT OURSELVES FROM SPIRITUAL/ENERGY ATTACKS?

• BUILDING A STRONG AURIC BODY

When someone sends negative energy to an individual it first starts affecting the outer energy layers of that person before reaching the physical body made of flesh and bones. It starts making holes in the aura and weakens it. When a person has a thick and strong layer of auric body the negative energy does not pierce through it easily and bounces back, it does not reach the physical body. It is very essential for each one of us to have a thick strong unbroken aura as the first step to building protection around us. When an individual is spiritually strong and has a solid faith connected with the divine they start building an unbroken aura which in return gradually makes the person physically strong with a better immune system and mentally more stable with a better hold of their emotions. This is possible by having a regular spiritual routine, practising a few things on a daily basis like some amount of meditation, chanting certain words or mantras which provide protection energy, using daily affirmations, facing your fears head on and most importantly maintaining a spiritual hygiene, which means being careful about who you let in your close circle. We cannot avoid certain people at professional settings as we need to hang around people for work but we can always have tall boundaries when it comes to your personal inner circle. Keeping energy vampires, toxic friends, narcissistic family members and low vibrational people at a distance is highly essential while building an impenetrable aura. Only once these people are out of your energy the broken aura starts building itself back, your energy stops leaking out and becomes thick.

• OPERATING FROM THE HIGHER MOST VI-BRATION POSSIBLE BY DEFAULT AT ALL TIMES

Everything has a frequency which is a certain number like every emotion, every food item and every space has a frequency, which can be higher or lower. If we consume foods that are of the lower frequency we start adding those lower numbers to ourselves and our average frequency gets lower and lower. Dead meat is a type of food that has the lowest frequency, close to zero, which means everytime we consume meat our average frequency of the body lowers. We tend to get nightmares, fear, anxiety and depression more when we consume meat because meat is full of those emotions, it retains all of those lower vibrations while kept in the slaughterhouse and during the process of slaughter. So naturally when we consume meat we will bring all of those vibrations into our body. Now because every emotion also has a frequency attached to it, like hate, anger, shame, pity, jealousy, confusion, guilt are all in the lower most zone with a very low number. Acceptance is the neutral space in the middle, and then comes Love after acceptance as we keep going up. We need to make sure that we are operating from the space of Love, Love as in not romantic but as Universal Unconditional Love by default everyday. It should be the vibration and number from which we make decisions, look at ourselves and others and create anything or do our work. That is a very good practice and an intentional effort that can be made to make sure that you are maintaining a high vibe at all times. It should be by default, without a question but that doesn't mean we lower our boundaries and let ourselves get exploited. You don't have to over give, over share or necessarily always show love to be in the state of love, it is just a state of being, feeling and existing. You are wrapped in the envelope of that high vibe.

Now you will ask me, "How does that help me to protect myself from negative energy attacks?". My answer to you will be that this universe is very huge where everything exists, good, bad, evil, angelic, lower demonic frequencies and higher divine frequencies as well. Everything exists but has its own space and dimension. Lower vibrations and lower entities always exist around us, but can they touch us, can they harm us is up to us. If any individual vibrates in the lower frequencies of greed, jealousy, hate and shame they will naturally align with the lower entities who are in the same zone and allow them to reach you. Because always remember whatever frequency you are at, you will attract that. On the other hand if you rise up and get yourself at the higher frequency zone you will not find lower entities in your life, you will only find beings, people, places and opportunities that are of the same high vibe as you. You will operate from the high vibe at all times and the low vibration entities, places will just pass under you without touching you. Even if anyone sends you negative energy on purpose it will fail to reach you due to the mismatch of the number. It's like a radio station, where you can tune in to that particular channel only if you know the frequency number, now if you keep dialing a wrong number you won't be able to connect with the right radio station. Similarly over here, all the evil eye and spell work doesn't reach the person but only bounces back to the sender. By remaining in a high vibe at all times we can be sure to remain protected even at the most uncertain situations. It requires one to be true to the meaning of being in that state, which means not consuming low vibrating content like false news, mindless humor, violence, excessive gore or horror, porn and emotionally abusive content etc. as the mental diet needs to be checked too, not entertaining any negative ideas, thoughts or mental desires also. With a certain amount of dedication and vigilance, it gradually transforms a person and makes a permanent shift in their life. It naturally becomes a default state of mind and being over a period of time. It should be a part of every one's upbringing and education where they are given this amount of information and guidance, post which the individual can choose their path and decide where they want to reside on the frequency chart.

The approach to having Unconditional Universal Love is a starter and the basic bare minimum to maintaining this frequency, as once we find ourselves steady and grounded in this state for a significant amount of time we can be sure to move high up on the chart to other positive and expansive states of Enlightenment, Bliss and Ultimate consciousness.

CHAPTER 5

MY MOTHER AND I NEMESIS DOPPLEGANGERS

ONE WAS TRYING TO BREAK THE GENERATIONAL CURSE AND THE OTHER WAS ACTIVELY LIVING THE CURSE AND ADDING TO IT

I was born into a completely dysfunctional family to a narcissistic mother who was appointed to sabotage my growth and break me because the enemy, the dark side of the universe, knew I was a Chosen One even before my birth, when I was in the womb. My mother tried all kinds of tricks and tactics to manipulate and break me upon witnessing some of my abilities as a child, like I have spoken about in the earlier chapters but she didn't have the understanding, the capability to handle a child like that. It's the energy of a person, a child, an animal or anybody that is recognized or felt by someone at various levels, consciously, subconsciously or just at a soul level. Whether you realize it or not, acknowledge it or not, you will feel their energy and you will notice its peculiarity and strangeness, even if they are an infant.

After my birth, while growing up in the early years, my mother noticed my good appearance, musical gifts and other talents. She encouraged me only to a point though, allowing me to shine but not beyond her. She was musically gifted just like me, but wasn't able to pursue music professionally because of getting married early and not taking initiative in it. Much later while things got very disturbing in the household she tried making attempts at physically hurting me, trying to cause serious physical injury. And even made attempts at taking my life. It was very evil, it was as if the enemy was working through her, possessing her vessel, constantly trying to stop my progress & break me even at that tender age.

It's very disturbing and sad to reveal these things, let it out loud like this and say it on record but it's true that she's an evil narcissistic person because of how unhealed she is.

She's 70 right now and even at this age she's so unhealed that negative entities, negative energies take control of her very easily and use her to harm other people.

I can't say what she did before me, as I wasn't there to see it, but after I was born I definitely saw her harm people, who were close and defenseless. Her heart chakra was blocked due to not being able to heal herself, she did not know how to receive and give love, how to reciprocate a positive interaction, how to have a motherly connection with her children. She saw her children as investments that she wanted to benefit from at regular intervals. She was harvesting energy from her children, using their accomplishments to receive recognition, validation, a certain status quo and using their energy to even stay youthful.

When it came to me she could sense the peculiarity, she could sense the rare energy of a Chosen one and she was very threatened by that. The negative energies though kept using her to harm me, humiliate me, break my confidence every chance they got in many ways since I can barely remember. It was a plan to sabotage me in every possible way, sabotage my growth, sabotage my talents, my gifts and attempts to take my life. It's very sad and depressing for all of you guys to read this, I am sure. These kinds of dark real life stories might be very new for a lot of you guys. She's not even my stepmother, she's my real mother, who has given birth to me, looks exactly like me, **she's my doppelganger** but she is completely consumed by the evil side. I was born to break the curse, I am the Chosen one to have understood the patterns, recognized the ancestral curses and I am destined to break every pattern, set myself free and start a new lineage, a new stream of bloodline which is healed and free of curse. I felt like my mother could have also broken these patterns if she wanted to, she was strong willed and had a powerful mind but she gave in and added to the patterns instead. She actively lived the curses and worked with the negative patterns to take me down because I was trying to break them.

I understood the entire dynamic only in the recent years when I was awakened spiritually. Gradually everything became transparent, I could read and see through the whole system of this meshwork, how various concepts were linked to one another. I was easily able to see the intense deep meaning of the connections & its traced back dots, which I was observing for decades anyway. We always wondered why mother was always so mean to people, we blamed it on her deep seated emotional issues, lack of financial independence and unfulfilled dreams & passions, but the problem was much deeper.

THE NATURE OF FULL BLOWN NARCISSISTS

She is a highly narcissistic woman also, not a coveted narcissist but a full-blown narcissist, who would show her negative side unapologetically, unhesitatingly while bragging about it.

These are the people who aren't aware that this behavior has been studied, identified and defined as sociopathic and narcissistic by psychologists, they are unaware that the world has identified and put a finger on them. They have a very entitled personality, where they think they can get away with anything and everything, and they never find themselves at fault. The other person is always at fault while they play the victim card at every opportunity and seek sympathy from those around them very desperately. They will attack another person by weaving a web of lies, fabricating crazy and unbelievable stories completely opposite to what that person actually is, to defame them, turn others against them, so that they miss out on work opportunities and suffer in interpersonal relationships. These full blown Narcs sometimes will go out of their way to attack your reputation, will resort to spell work, negative energy work, evil eyeing and even plot on attacking you physically if they decide to destroy you. They will leave no stone unturned incase they consider you their enemy and make it their mission to watch you fall. It all stems from jealousy and their deep seated insecurities about themselves. Remember they dont love themselves either, they won't work on their own happiness, they won't do any kind of self developing activity, any kind of spiritual inner healing activity, inner work, shadow work, connecting with their emotional body, accepting grief, crying it out, practising forgiveness etc. They won't even believe that they need any amount of physical and mental betterment because they are delusional enough to think that they are completely fine, they are at their best, they don't need to fix anything about themselves and only other people need to fix themselves. Which is why they never get better and never rise above any situation, they remain at that same emotional and spiritual level forever. If they are hurt over a certain situation, years will pass by but they won't be able to move on. If they felt some kind of loss 10 years ago, they will still keep feeling that loss even at the present time because they just don't know how to let go, unless there arises a new and bigger issue in front of them. Only then can they distract themselves and look away in another direction for sometime. You will notice that other people around them would have risen, moved on and graduated to higher levels of understanding and expansion in their professions, spiritually, mentally etc. But these people will still be stuck in their old paradigm, in their old mindsets because they wont stop living that life. They will choose to stay bitter by talking about those difficult situations, by bringing up those people again and again in their conversations, by still holding onto their anger, rage, the need for revenge, the need to show their false superiority as a facade while they are feeling deeply inferior inside. And because they see you move on so fast, they see you upgrading every time they try and want to keep you stuck at their level with them, they want to bring you down to their level. They want to revive the old you who was dealing and accepting their narcissistic ways. We know that misery likes company, right? So because they are miserable they want you to be miserable as well so you can give them company, which is why they can't stand another person's happiness. It's very sad. It doesnt let them heal and keeps them stuck on a disastrous loop of life. Over the years you will notice them looking older and weaker, they could even attract some ailments, like liver, stomach diseases, nervous system issues because of all the pent up negative energy which breeds inside them, literally reproducing inside them. That will slowly start eating them up from within, from inside out. Because they show a fake strong facade to the outside world while they are getting weaker by the day on the inside, they won't accept defeat, their ego won't let them accept help of any kind and they are really foolish enough to not even heal by themselves. It is a state of passive self harm, self deterioration and bitterness to the whole wide world. They cannot see anything beautiful in this world, they keep their eyes wide open to only find negativity in this world, only find faults with other people and turn everything pretty into a disaster. A lot of times you will notice the extremity of their misfortune, I would say their blinding ego and God complex which doesnt let them appreciate anything good around them or keep the blessings they receive. God brings miracles, fortune and blessings to them too in the form of people, opportunities, gifts, talents but they somehow can't keep these blessings for long. Their inherent energy seeks chaos and drama, they don't like being in peace for too long, they can't stay in the state of harmony for too long, they like to get out of that state often and seek drama through unnecessary conflict with people. They pick silly fights, petty quarrels and turn them into serious issues which they will then brood upon for long. Even when the other person gives up and forgets the whole matter to rise above it and find peace, the full blown narcissist on the other hand has taken it to another imaginary competitive level, converted their mind into a battlefield and declared an imaginary war against that person. Mind it, all of this is happening in their heads, they deal with delusions of many levels everyday. Narcissists are extremely delusional 90% of their time, they live in their own world unaware and indifferent to any other perspective. They will surround themselves with 'yes men', people who believe their lies, who gas them up. When they go out of their way to hurt someone they will do a detailed research and background study of the other person's past, present etc. They will even contact your support system, close friends and family etc to turn them against you. Like I said they will go to great extents and put all their energy to bring your downfall. They might involve others in a smear campaign and engage in it for months but soon the others come to know how delusional their entire plan is, because their delusional stories, fabricated lies always fall short of any proof. They never get enough evidence to back their theories because the way they describe the other person's character in the smear campaigns, it's completely the opposite of what the person actually is.

THE DANGERS OF HAVING AN EMPATH CHILD TO A NARCISSISTIC PARENT

It is a very very dangerous combination when you have an empath and a narcissist under the same roof. This is a relationship dynamic that I had to endure all my childhood. Here the narcissist is going to use the empath in very dangerous ways even if the empath is your own child, they won't behave any differently. In fact the abuse will be more because they will consider their child as their property and will feel entitled to treat them however they want.

When you're a child you literally are very vulnerable and inexperienced as a being, you're incapable of protecting yourself outside and inside the house. You don't know anything about what's going on in this world and that is what the narcissist takes advantage of. They are predators in the form of a parent in the 3D realm. And in the spiritual realm they are agents on assignment sent by the enemy disguised as parents.

The narcissist parent is going to mould you, manipulate you, break you, burn you and do everything in their power to keep you from developing and experiencing your gifts and if nothing works out ultimately they will also try to end your life. I really don't understand how I survived this whole phase of mine, my entire childhood, I have no explanations but I can only point my finger to God, that only God could have helped me survive through this whole thing. It was my connection with the spirit, my ancestors, my angel guides. Literally the divine has the entire credit of protecting me and saving me and keeping me alive so that I can tell the story out loud at this point of life. The kind of things that I was inflicted upon I could have easily left earth on more than a couple of occasions.

To destroy my life and keep me a nobody while harnessing my energy as a supply to their wellbeing was the intention of my family from the beginning, to sort of let me fade away with time without blooming into my power as they were not happy with how different I was from them. When you're strikingly different from your family, when you embody a completely different energy, when you just don't blend in with your family, you are seen as a black sheep in their eyes. You actually don't belong there and they don't know what to do with you, they don't know what to do to you. They want to break you strategically by misunderstanding you on purpose and put you in a corner so you can perish by yourself. But that doesn't happen for Chosen Ones, as they are very much protected by the Universe due to their good heart, **they survive all the abuse and live until one day when they heal themselves and tell their story to the world.**

I was gaining my strength over the years gradually as I was getting into my teen years, my adolescence, I was changing slowly, feeling a fresh sense of freedom everytime I stepped out of the house, appealed by my new found interests, friends, fun and frolic. My sense of self, sense of freedom and sovereignty was developing rapidly along with my God given sharp physical appearance. I was blooming into womanhood, experiencing new emotions, the newfound interest in the opposite sex and exploring the deepest parts of myself. Started developing more power and a sense of self about me and little did I know it was already a huge threatening situation to my mother. I entered my teens barely 13 14 15 years of age and I was a huge sign of impedance to the narcissistic parent to a point where they were not able to handle my presence anymore. Constant events were orchestrated at home to humiliate me, my mother urging my dad to exercise more control on me, using their authority to make compromising decisions for me. Luckily after a couple of years I had to leave home for higher studies after my high school. Thank GOD! and that helped me survive big time, it was in my destiny to leave home early, not stay with the family in the family home and ultimately never go back to them. It was part of my life plan because unless I did that I would not grow in my own way, I would be completely burnt out, brainwashed and shattered into pieces by their attacks, manipulative attempts etc.

So it was part of my destiny to leave home early and sort of never go back which has really happened. For the last 20 years I've been by myself, since the time I've left home for my under graduation. Of course I've lived in community spaces like college hostels, or as a paying guest during my undergraduation, post graduation and the times between. I never felt the need to depend on family, never felt the need to because there was no form of dependency earlier anyway apart from the parental financial support. I never missed anything else, the emotional, mental and spiritual guidance barely existed.

A BLOODLINE OF POWERFUL PSYCHIC PRIESTS AND PRIESTESSES

I come from a blood line of very psychic people, a bloodline of very spiritually powerful people which is why I have that calibre in my blood too. Along with these gifts this bloodline also carries a lot of curses, toxic patterns in relationships, certain low vibrational mindsets and diseases of some kinds. The bloodline coming from my mothers side carries a lot of trauma, a colossal amount of generational trauma all trickling down generations after generations. My ancestors, both male and female, suffered a lot when they were alive hundreds and thousands of years ago due to their own doings. These people were influential with their spiritual knowledge, psychic and healing abilities, most of them used these gifts for the greater good of the community while some got greedy. They began using their gifts in the wrong way, for the wrong reasons and turned into oppressors, who began abusing their knowledge and authority, exploiting innocent people and the community at large for their own material gains and advantage. There are good and bad ancestors basically right, so the wicked ancestors and their lineages reigned for a long time, they accumulated a lot of karma in that process, they attracted a lot of curse, a lot of bad omen. They promoted slavery, committed adultery of the worst kinds, were involved in various other crimes etc. In this way they made the Gods angry, their spiritual ranks, divine abilities and blessings were taken away by the Universe, slowly misfortune followed them, the bad karma was a lot for it to get balanced easily, these curses and patterns kept trickling down the generations, from hundreds of years. People in these families are still paying off the karma of their ancestors, carrying the misfortune in their fate, the negative ethos in their psyche and living the toxic patterns, trying to pass it down to their children.

CHAPTER 6

THE BODY JUMPING PHENOMENON

HOW EVIL ENTITIES 'JUMP BODIES' TO ATTACK CHOSEN ONES

Similar Analogy to the movie 'The Matrix'

If you have watched 'The Matrix' and the next couple of parts of that movie series you will get this concept easily. In the Matrix movie the character Agent Smith and his colleagues keep appearing in other human bodies of the 3D matrix to attack their targets over and over again. Even when the Agents get shot they don't die, they pause for a while, they slow down but very quickly they track the target's location and reappear in another human body who is in that location. It's like them getting teleported instantly and taking over another person's mind and body, controlling it completely, using that body as a device or a vehicle to reach their targets. If you haven't seen the Matrix or you had watched it long ago, I would suggest you watch it again in this era, as you will watch it with a fresh pair of eyes with upgraded understanding this time. You will grasp this concept wholly once you experience the movie, because it is exactly what they were trying to explain and it really happens in the real world. It happens to Chosen Ones, like Neo in the movie who is also a Chosen One. The Agents dont come at everyone, they only come after the ones who are plugged out of the matrix, who have awakened to the reality of the matrix and are working hard towards awakening others through their work. They understand the difference between a fake life which is programmed and the reality which exists only out of the matrix. In this programmed life you are asked and expected to do the same mundane things everyday, follow rules made by others which don't help you and waste away all of your precious time, waste your life away without ever using your brain much, without asking any questions to anyone and actually without even living your life properly. Take a look at the older generations, a lot of people in your previous generations who succumbed to the slavery of mind and body. During their time the veil was way too thick, there was way too much suffering and captivity in every sense where everyone was working hard to make ends meet. No one could think beyond the matrix, as that would mean cutting out the options of survival. People were in desperate times, in the survival mode throughout, generations after generations since hundreds of years. Even now a lot of families are stuck in that mindset due to the trauma stored in their blood, even if the current generation of those bloodlines want to free themselves, they find it very difficult to overcome the mindset in the first place, to be able to feel deserving of any form of freedom which could lead to ultimate breakage of the matrix at an individual level. That happens because we are still so connected with the ideologies of our ancestors, our parents who live with us are unable to provide an environment which is free from those thoughts and patterns. The level of fear, doubt and anxiety is so high that it is bound to penetrate any mind which dwells in that environment. There is a saying, 'You cannot heal yourself in the same environment that hurt you'. It is extremely essential to remove yourself from the environment which gave you trauma if you want to heal yourself. Every environment is attached to certain memories, emotions and energies, which do not allow you to change by keeping you trapped in the old frequency. But some of us are able to understand the game, the game of this matrix, some of us are able to see it like a game, the programming, the lies and the brainwashing very clearly. Just like how Neo saw it, which is why he was called the 'Anomaly'. The programs don't end at being the systems in place or the rules and obligations placed by the grid at large. The people who place these regulations, by laws and systems are programs themselves. While we are operating in the matrix you will have to abide by some of the regulations, as without it survival can still be difficult. But as an awakened individual you will need to know when and where to draw the line. There has to be a line at some point, you can allow the regulations till the public domain but you must be very aware when it comes to your personal life, your personal space and decisions. You cannot allow an outsider to regulate what happens in your house, in your body and in your mind. Personal things like what you wear, what you eat, what is your mindset, what your lifestyle choices, what are your standards and your definition of anything, like your definition of success, your definition of wealth, youth, freedom, happiness and your equation with the world etc. Those are extremely personal and individual parameters, where you cannot allow the world's regulations to enter. For example if something is declared crazy by the world, in the matrix, but you don't consider it crazy. For you it is very normal and absolutely general. Then you must continue your life with the same perspective and not bother about the worldly parameters. When you do so you are not allowing the matrix regulation to enter your mind, you don't have to fight with anyone about it, you don't have to argue with anyone, you are quiet about it and simply live unfazed and unaffected. Here, you chose to use your discernment and stood your ground, you held space for your psyche and personal mindset without making a big deal about it. Which is why as a Chosen one we will need to use discernment, we will need to look at what is required from the matrix and what is not. Things which are unnecessary, which waste your time and energy, which force you to abandon yourself, regulations that dont help you in any way but are rather placed to take your freedom away and break your will power and individuality will need to be kept aside. Because the system cannot really force you to do anything, it just uses the programs, the Agents to make you feel isolated, stranded, like an outcast and finally talk you out of your own decisions. The system cannot enter your personal space unless you allow it, the control is in your hand, but it's like we give away the control ourselves. We hand over the remote control to them ourselves and then ask them to control us, tell us what we should do, when we already know what we should do, when we already know what we want to do. How do you know what you should do? Your 'Intuition' has all the answers, it's been telling you what is your purpose, what you should do all along since a long time, but we have not heard it or paid any attention to it. The Voice of your intuition is not loud enough because of being ignored for a long time. But once you start listening to it you will know what is right for you and what you actually need to do.

The Chosen ones who have awakened in their lifetime due to many hardships, self mastery and divine intervention will be able to see past the veil, the manipulation, the hollow promises and the strategic traps clear as day. Self mastery begins in isolation, it is a forced separation by the universe to cut out the external noise and create an opportunity to go within. Even after the much initial struggle the Chosen aways sees the reason and privilege behind it at some point and finally gives into the process.

The negative energies find hosts in a low vibrational place, situation or person. They cannot use a high vibrational awakened person as a host, because of the overall mismatch. There is always a high risk of opening up and giving access to a negative energy i.e. an agent at social gatherings and frequent outdoor activities being exposed to all kinds of people. Which is why the Chosen has to choose isolation for better protection of their being and energy. It is preferred for constant recharging, efficient use of their energy without unwanted wastage and compromise. A lot of these people in disguise wearing masks keep approaching the Chosen at various timelines of their life, just to keep distracting them from their focus, delaying them from reaching their goals and making them go in circles trying to keep them trapped in karmic cycles. They use emotions, mutual work etc and try to own or control parts of you very early on in the connection, they try very hard to break those boundaries and get into the inner circle to figure out your mysteries, unravel your future hidden plans and your important information through sly conversations and a fake well wishing demeanour. They regularly spy on you because you don't give many hints, they cannot figure you out, your mystery is too irresistible to them. The negative energy seeks to know about your future plans only to hinder its progress and talk you out of your own potential. As soon as the Chosen figures out the dark agenda of their friend and cuts out the connection, not very long after, rather soon the negative energy approaches the Chosen again through another host. Another occupied host is sent in the form of a work, friend, romantic prospect or family. It almost has the same pattern, same energy and similar events start unfolding yet again in the same sequence. Yes, these jumps can happen with your family members too, basically anyone who operates in the lower frequencies of hate, anger, shame, pity, guilt, lack, depression, over indulgence, narcissists, abusers and the list goes on. Basically people who are in a negative state of mind most of their time and see the world with that lens.

ANECDOTES OF BODY JUMPING ENTITIES

These were those crazy times, if I have to explain the concept with a bit of my own story. My parents were living in Bangalore, India then 15 yrs ago, I was not living with them but I would visit them every week. Like I've mentioned before in the previous chapters, there was this negative energy following my family all the time. It was attached to them, wherever they went, it followed them. These negative energies had always used them as a host, especially my mother. My brother as well. So as they moved to Bangalore, the negative energies naturally came along with them and lived with them. It's like the vibe of the person. My mother was never positive, always complaining, always finding faults with everything. She never had one fun moment and never let anyone around her have a fun moment because of how frustrated she was with her life I guess. Being a housewife, doing chores everyday, not having financial independence, not having any of her dreams fulfilled. You eventually become a bitter person. Ever since I knew her she was a bitter person in general. And it was in her fate where negative energy never left her. It was her own doing where she was always so sad and that she needed to hurt everyone around her to get some relief. Everytime I went to their place to visit them in Bangalore also, I would sense this negative energy all the time. There was never a pleasant moment where they sat down together and had lunch together or spent some time watching TV together in peace. Although they would expect me to be there, I never felt welcomed, it was very frustrating, it felt very forced. And sometimes the moments were very bad. Sometimes things would be worse, with fights, blame games, quarrels and intense negative energy in the air. Even in that short meeting of a couple of hours, in such a small visit, we would end up fighting, crying and me leaving their place in a bad mood. Mostly because she was very frustrated with her insecurities and was never grateful about anything she had. She complained about the house that they were living in, how small it was, in a not so great locality with loud neighbors. She always felt like she never got the life that she deserved. She kept saying she deserved more servants, like she had in her dads place, more money or a better lifestyle. She had to always find faults with whatever my dad offered and made him feel like he had fallen short of providing what she deserved. Although my dad is quite well off and has taken care of us. He has given us everything that he never had. I mean, you know, we are some of the well off people in our larger extended family. Like we are on the better side. But my mom never saw that as enough. She saw that as still very less. It was her own inadequacies deep inside that she projected on all of us, making us look and feel inadequate, although we were doing just fine. We lived in her projections all our lives. That was her perception of viewing everything, as the glass half empty, it was her thing, a scarcity mindset. And she compared herself to other people. She compared her life to mine too. I was living with my boyfriend in a large duplex with a couple of dogs and she was here living with my dad and everybody in a rented tiny flat which was way too small for so many people. Somehow she felt ashamed of that even in front of her own daughter. Basically all kinds of inner demons and unnecessary comparisons were at play.

This particular thing would happen after most of my visits with them. This very heavy dark cloud sort of energy would hover around me. After the fight I would slowly leave, walk out and then catch a cab or something and then go home. As soon as I left the house, I would be in a bitter and frighteningly angry state, while the dark cloud followed me.

That is what I saw a lot of times.

The whole experience would drag me down, big time, drag me down to a feeling so low, feeling so hurt, threatened, scared, angry and insecure all at the same time, like, you know, even revengeful.

I would sense the utter low vibes.

And exactly at this time I would walk out on the street, I would literally see the negative energy follow me, from my parents house. A part of it, a soul fraction of it would follow me on the street and appear through strangers on the street. Suddenly a passerby would say something very weird to me and just walk away. Like eve tease me in the most horrible way, make any physical gesture, give an extremely weird stare which would really tick me off, trigger me further into more anger. You can see the ugliness, the evilness in those people, the demon speaks through them even if for those few moments. Like when a regular person is possessed by the agents in the movie Matrix, they lose their original self and start taking orders from the entity that has possessed them even if it's for a few hours. After the entity leaves them they might not even remember what they had done or spoken earlier. An entirely different mind with different intentions takes control of that brain, that vessel. That negative energy, that agent, that bad energy, which was trying to trigger you and get a reaction out of you and try to hurt you so bad, the exact same energy. I can recognize it effortlessly because I would have just seen that same energy on my mom's face. I just saw it and felt it, felt its presence in that house while I was there, right? And as I keep walking it appears again in another person a hundred metres later, it just would not just stop chasing. After some time when you take a cab, you see that same face in the cab driver. That has happened to me many times now that I look back and connect the dots. And each and every time that I experienced that phenomena I had just dealt with a narcissist, had a huge fight and left the place, I can remember the years, back in 2004, 2012, 2023. It was the same pattern, but with different people. It was a narcissistic ex in 2004, a narcissistic mother in 2012 and a very toxic group of friends in 2023. These are just a few I am jotting down for the record, but there were many more such exact incidents to give me this understanding. The worst is when you have to deal with this energy in a cab driver all the way home, you don't want to cancel the ride, or ask him to stop. You are scared hoping he won't take you to another place. the entire way back, you are going to have to see that man's face while he keeps muttering something. These incidents have happened to me many times, not once or twice, which is why I'm so sure and can describe it so well.

ANECDOTE OF 2023

The latest one that happened in 2023, it was a very unexpected event after ages, these incidents had stopped happening to me as I was being more careful about letting various people into my presence. I was away from family for years and had not allowed any negative energies or interactions in my life. But during that period I had moved in with my parents for a couple of months as a trial period trying to gauge my level of compatibility with them. They were growing old and I wanted to be there for them while not ignoring my physical and mental safety. Just a couple of days before this incident I had a huge ordeal at home with my mother, very unexpected. It was one of the worst fights ever, the one where my mom called the cops on me. I have mentioned this anecdote briefly in chapter 3,'My Childhood' of this book. To calm and distract myself I went over to a close friend's place, who I considered like a sister. But things were very different this time, I didn't realise she had been keeping immature company with bad habits and unhealthy lifestyle. Under their influence she had changed and had less control over her own judgements. We were up all night and the vibe got more and more dark as the night passed. We were under the influence of some herbs and my intuition was wide open. I could literally see the amount of hate, jealousy and discomfort they felt due to my presence. Just with how much I was enjoying my time and was expressing it with my dance. They tried giving me negative energy all night just to ruin my good trip and put me in a place of spiritual vulnerability. I could see it all. It was a very ugly situation where I had to literally block her off from all social media platforms the next week. I couldn't see her as a friend anymore. Although I used to think of her like a sister. I did help her out financially and emotionally a lot during her bad times but that night she crossed a line. It was like the negative energy got to her very bad. It was all everywhere. I was not feeling good. I was really tormented all night. I was nearly shattered that night. It was a tough night. I was trying so hard to put myself together, bring my scattered bits and pieces together and feel normal. I kept saying to myself, 'All of this doesn't matter, it is just a test of my strength. I cannot lash out on anyone but only learn how to transmute it'. But I held it together no matter what, protected myself thoroughly as much as I could and transmuted all of that energy into strength for the next morning. I couldn't leave their place at night because I had a few classes to take early in the morning which I had planned in that way.

While leaving their place in the morning, the negative energy wasn't ready to leave, it first appeared as a weird man trying to come close while I waited for the cab and then I caught a cab and the cab driver had that face. It was like a deja vu, I can just recognize the agent's energy everytime. He started saying some weird malicious stuff, the low vibe was oozing out of his being. I was in utter shock, somewhat scared but held it together until I reached my destination. Avoided any conversations or eye contact with him although he kept trying to ask many questions. I somehow managed to complete the ride and get on with the day. That was again another experience that confirmed the theory. That is how we attract things. If we are in the low vibe, you are going to attract a low vibe person in your next interaction. Because of the huge episode with my mother I was put in an extremely negative zone, which in return kept bringing me to the evil side of people, friends etc. Negative spiritual entities were able to show up more frequently while creating negative experiences. Evil entities jumping from one spot to another around you, it happens more when we are in the lowest of the vibrations. You will remain unaffected by it if you vibe higher. Basically it won't be able to latch onto you or your environment because it does not support it. I believe that my friends were in a very low vibe overall and that night it all came to surface and started throwing it at me because I was vibing low too. It just found a match, it found support and started functioning out loud, which otherwise were dormant.

I was indeed very proud of myself for staying up all night, battling all the demons in a hallucinogenic state when you are more vulnerable than usual, going through shit again in the morning and then staying put to take a few classes right after in that state of mind. I displayed some next level spiritual and mental strength which I didn't know I had. I had reached a certain level and gained some rank that night.

So body jumping is a very, very common thing which happens for the Chosen people. It can jump from a family member to a stranger to a cabbie to a friend and all the way even to the other side on a phone call. Its purpose is to knock you off your own stable high vibe and drag you down to feeling all other lower emotions. To hurt you so badly that you don't get up to fulfill your tasks or have the courage to even face anyone. To break your confidence and sense of self. So basically when this happens, the first thing is to not give in to those emotions of fear, anger, worthlessness and depression. Just observe it and walk away. Do not engage in it and or internalize it to make it a part of your inner world. Just look at it as an experience and end it right there. Do not take it home, to your head or to your bed where you sleep.

Body jumping is like a phenomenon that we need to be aware of. It's just like 'The Matrix'.

If you watch the Matrix movie, you will know what I'm talking about. It is just like that. I really don't know how but I am really amused, surprised and absolutely blown away thinking that the makers of the Matrix knew about this two decades ago. I mean, I wonder what all they have experienced, how much do they know then, what all do they know about this whole thing because they were able to explain these things so clearly and able to make a revolutionary path breaking movie about these realities, about these crazy phenomena two decades ago, which I have experienced all my life but have been able to join the dots and comprehend only now with the help of the content of many other Chosen Ones and the Movie. I did not understand the movie Matrix when it came 20 years ago, I never questioned it even. But recently I watched all four parts suddenly, while writing this book as if I was being called to watch it out of nowhere.

I was kind of not well during the time of writing this chapter, I think I had some spare time while recovering and I binge watched all four parts in two days. Man, it cleared so many things again one more time. I was able to watch the movies with a fresh pair of eyes and a brand new understanding as I am a different person now, more advanced and experienced. I was like shit man these are the things I go through. These are the exact plots of my life too.

HOW TO PROTECT OUR ENERGY FROM BODY JUMPING ENTITIES AND MONITORING SPIRITS?

So that is how it is and which is why the Chosen Ones are always forced to choose isolation so that they don't waste their time dealing with these bodies, with these entities that are constantly jumping. It's a waste of time. I mean you can always combat them, you can fight them, you can understand their tricks and you know how to protect yourself and everything but it's going to simply waste your time, waste your energy. It's going to take away huge chunks of energy every time you meet a negative entity.

- **ISOLATION IS KEY**

Every time you encounter these kinds of people and trust me they won't stop coming.

They're going to keep coming maybe till the end of your life, till your last breath because the negative energy is never dying right. They always exist so they will try to keep sending you people, bodies, hosts at different times of your life through all kinds of circumstances.

It will try to seek a gap, wherever it sees a gap it will try to fit in as that respective connection or relation. **The key is to not ever give it the gap, the gap is basically a need or a desperation, the key is us not feeling the need or desperation for people, connections or personal relationships. We must learn to feel content in Isolation because that keeps us protected. Then there is little to no scope of any body jumping entity damaging your inner temple as they are not a part of your inner personal circle.** When a genuine connection comes you will recognise and accept it. It will be a high vibe God sent connection which won't get tampered by the lower entities. You need to wait for that. Till then if you can avoid random people, low vibrational people, unnecessary connections, people approaching without any solid reason it will benefit you. Avoid even low vibrational settings, environments, conversations where it's more likely that you will find such people. For example environments where alcohol is involved, other substances and dark practices are involved. Exposing yourself to such settings is a high risk situation and it can pull in evil entities to you almost immediately. These entities will be attracted to the Chosen Ones undoubtedly and the environment also will support them to get activated and function towards you. God, universe, the Most High is going to force you to learn the art of being alone until you have done some healing work on yourself, until you learn the hard lessons.

Dear Chosen, you did not come here to just wake up in the morning, eat, sleep, go to work, come back, watch TV and do what everybody else is doing. That's not what you came here to do, you came here for a greater purpose. These are your lessons from the universe, if you're still very thirsty for relationships, you want a commitment with someone, want somebody to be around you all the time, you will need to break out of it. You do not need anyone, I can promise you that, I've been on my own for years, I wake up, I do my thing, I do what I am supposed to do without expectations or questions, I create, I produce, I build, help whoever needs my wisdom, do my spiritual practices alone and with the community, help the planet ascend as a whole, make my dollars, communicate with the Most High and go back to sleep. That is what you're here to do, you did not come here to get into entanglements that do not serve you. You had your share of fun, friends, family etc when you were younger, that could have been good or bad according to what you needed, but there is no need to repeat that again in this stage of your life. You must learn the art of being alone, wait till the most high sends you the right partner, as this particular person also will be a Chosen like you, who vibrates high like you. That person is also going to be protected the same way that you are because these relationships are Divine and they are protected by the Divine. Only then you will be happy in that connection, it will be a God ordained connection. Every other connection will be karmic, will cause you stress and only delay your purpose. Every other connection will not be able to handle your star power, your gifts. They will always be threatened by your anointing. They will envy you everyday and cause obstacles in your success, in your purpose. They will always try to dim your light because only then they can appear a match to you. Do not continue yearning and thirsting for relationships when you know you have not found the right one or your purpose in life. Because when the right one comes along you will know. Till then don't focus on relationships or seek companions just for the sake of spending some time, it is only wasting your limited time on earth, focus on healing, on finding your life purpose and then start working on it vigorously. Like I have mentioned earlier, these attacks and body jumps wont stop. Yes you are reading it right, if you are a Chosen, these attacks won't stop till the end, they will try attacking you every single chance they get. They will try to bring confusion, distraction, create delays, change your course of life and bring in destruction so that you don't fulfil your purpose and reach your destination on time. Hence, you need to make your own strategy and play clever. The more you look for companions, you are only giving them more chances to body jump and attack you through those companions who are only being used as vessels. Lovers and relationships are the easiest way to attack because this is where we become our most vulnerable selves, we become intimate physically and emotionally. We sort of open all our sacred chambers and our mind to them, we expose our raw selves, pull down all the defences and guards.

We share our deepest secrets, pains, joys, weaknesses, fears and give them all the tools through which they can formulate all forms of attacks on us.

• MAINTAIN A REGULAR CONNECTION WITH GOD & HIGHER POWERS

This is the sole reason why Chosen Ones are kept away from the matrix and hidden in plain sight by their spirit guides. You will see Chosen Ones kept in forced isolation by the universe, tucked away in a secluded village or in some spot where no one can see them, no one can find them. Even their family won't know where they live, a lot of people would be removed from their life mainly because there is a distinct frequency mismatch. They're available only on social media and even if they're seen online there will be an energetic wall, a boundary around them that would make them inaccessible.

There will be this energetic wall which will always stop people from approaching them, connecting with them unnecessarily. People will think 5 times before asking them anything. It's that **energetic signature** that you have which demands people to think 10 times before asking you anything or even commenting on your post. And it is divinely done, divinely programmed, it is a part of divine protection. To make sure of your divine protection and to strengthen it, we need to connect with the divine, the source on a regular basis in some form. It can be meditation, prayers, moon rituals, affirmations etc. God is there to protect you but you will also need to make efforts to maintain that connection. You will sense the protection getting stronger with time. It is done by the divine because it is required in that manner. So that you don't have to encounter these body jumps.

They will of course let you experience it, make you experience the body jumping phenomena enough number of times in your early or 1st half of your life so that you are aware of it and can recognise it. If it occurs again you will immediately recognise the energy and take necessary steps. Inexperienced individuals will never come to know of this whole thing and won't be aware of it when it happens. So it will happen enough times for you while you are under protection till you get a thorough understanding of it. These are the training periods, getting you ready to go into the 3D matrix and perform your tasks tactfully. Trust me I have been in training since I was a child. You can recognize the negative energy right away as soon as you see it in another body, you recognize the face, you see the pattern, you immediately know what's going to happen next, you can predict the pattern and before anything happens you can cut it out and rush back.

• MAINTAIN A HIGH FREQUENCY AT ALL TIMES

If you have gone through the emotional frequency chart you will understand the various human emotions and their respective frequency. If you haven't seen it, just type in google images, **'Emotional Frequency Chart'** and you will see a rainbow colored chart which starts at **'alpha'** at the bottom tip where the color is red and gradually gets broader, the top is broad which ends at **'omega'** where the color is violet.

The colors have a great significance here which align with the seven chakras of a human being. Starting with the first chakra, called the **'root chakra'** which sits at the base of our spine is red in color. And the seventh chakra which is called the **'crown chakra'** sits above our head and is violet in color. These chakras are seen in one straight line when a person is sitting or standing straight. The sequence of these colors are just like the sequence of a rainbow. The root chakra is responsible for the stability of our survival emotions, it mostly deals with the primal emotions of fear, shame, guilt, lust, earthly competition and sustenance. All these emotions are at the least frequency, at zero or 20hz. It's about the connection with earth, how grounded we are and how we can use our primal instincts in a positive way. It is red because it denotes emotions like passion, anger and desire. When this chakra is open, active, flowing and working right, you'll feel grounded and comfortably situated in your body and the world around you. Stress about your sense of place and belonging will dissipate. While when this chakra is blocked your well-being can suffer. The root chakra acts as the root of the body. If your root chakra is out of alignment, you may feel depressed, anxious and even suicidal because you lose the connection with earth and your being no longer wants to inhabitate earth. This is when the negative energies find you as an easy prey and feed off of your insecurities, fear and anxiety. They can easily possess your mind and thoughts in this state and make you speak wrong things or take actions to harm others and yourself.

Now coming to our point of maintaining a high vibe, as you progress along the emotional frequency chart, you will cross all the negative emotions and somewhere in the middle you reach acceptance which is in the green area. And beyond acceptance there is understanding, love and gratitude. These emotions fall in the bluish zone which is basically aligning with the **'throat chakra'** sitting in our throat and the **'third eye chakra'** between both our eyes. We need to make sure that we operate from these emotions of love, gratitude and acceptance at all times by default. The frequency of these emotions are at 500Hz. This is the minimum level everyone should maintain. It is not easy initially but with practice and continued effort one can achieve this state because you start looking at yourself, others and the world around you through your third eye, the sixth chakra in a human body. When your third eye is open and active it shows you many other spiritual aspects that exist beyond the veil. You start realising that everything, all good and bad that has happened, was ultimately happening for you and not to you. You start connecting many dots of your past and present, understand things in a much deeper way and eventually come to the state of acceptance. Gradually from the state of acceptance you move to the other higher emotions of love, joy and bliss again with conscious effort, dedication and self mastery. It is very easy to fall back, slip off on these journeys because the 3D world around you is always going to try throwing a wrench in your wellbeing machinery, try stopping your deep inner work and drag you back down to the lower emotions. But it is up to an individual, their level of strength and perseverance that will be tested by the world multiple times but if they remain fortified and understand the game well they can certainly climb up the emotional frequency chart and beat any lower entity. An individual at this point needs to know themselves in and out and accordingly churn out a plan which works for them. Every individual is different, certain lifestyle changes may or may not work in their favour. But once you know yourself thoroughly you will understand what keeps you in a high vibe, what are the activities, foods and environments that help you maintain that vibe of love and gratitude. And once you have cracked those along with a plan you just need to follow it with discipline and dedication, and upgrade it every year or whenever you are nudged intuitively.

CHAPTER 7

WHAT HAPPENS? AS THE CHOSEN ONE BREAKS THE GENERATIONAL CURSE

These are a few things that will start happening in the bloodline over a period of a few years when the Chosen One breaks the Generational Curses and Ancestral toxic patterns and slowly moves out of the family system. Like we have discussed earlier, the generational patterns are passed on to us from our very old ancestors, going back to 7-8 generations. The patterns keep on repeating generation after generation as none of the new parents or children see a fault in it. They fail to spot any dysfunctions or malfunctioning cycles and consider it regular, a part of their normal system. They do not try to change anything because it is comfortable for them to live in the dysfunctions. Even if they sometimes notice that some things are annoying and it pinches their skin, they still dont stand up to it or raise a voice against it. They don't feel the need for it, most of the time they wonder, who are they to make those changes? Why should they in the first place?

105

Why will anyone listen to them? Is their voice even bold enough? Are their reasons even valid enough? Are they even that strong and powerful to stand against the authority figures of their own family? All these doubts keep hovering over their entire life and they end up always giving in to the patterns, never being able to look in the eyes of these dysfunctions and ask it to stop once and for all. In the due course of time they allow these evil ways to keep repeating over and over again for decades and centuries without having the strength to call it out and remove it from their life and their children's lives.

This is when a Chosen One is sent to that family by the divine, these are children who are born out of a very important and divine purpose. The black sheeps are children who are actually sent to those families by the divine. The very reason why the black sheep turns out to become the Chosen One is because these children are sent by the universe. These children are supposed to come at that time and intercept that pattern, they're supposed to break the toxic patterns and break the curse with their energy. Just their energy, their presence and their destined way of being will be enough to break those patterns and free the entire bloodline. They will have innate courage and strong morals to implement changes which the other members of the bloodline had lacked.

1. THESE ARE BORROWED SOULS, THEY ARE VOLUNTEERS

They come to Earth to tell a different story. They are souls who are borrowed from other Star Systems, from other timelines, both future and past timelines, very advanced ancient civilizations who practised advanced technology, energy healing, medicine and ways of living when they were living in those systems, timelines and long lost lands. When you are in their presence, a lot of times you will feel like you are in a different era, in a different zone. The time-line sort of starts collapsing in front of you, you feel timeless and spaceless suddenly. That is because of their interdimensional cosmic energy which they display very much on the forefront. It makes everything float around you. Their energy will seem otherworldly and out of place but that is done on purpose by the divine because only an energy completely different than the existing bloodline will be able to make the changes effortlessly. It is an energy from outside, they are an outsider far from the bloodline, which is why they will never fit in. They are not meant to.

2. BORN WITH VERY POWERFUL PLANET PLACEMENTS IN THEIR BIRTH CHART

The planets in their birth chart align to a certain combination, a certain match which is exactly required for that child's destiny. The birth chart is nothing but a snapshot of how the planets were placed at the time of anyone's birth. A lot of times you will find Rahu and Ketu, (which is the north node and south node of the Moon respectively) in very important positions of their birth chart.

Rahu, the north node, is a shadow planet that makes the individual a differentiator, provides them the raw courage to question each and everything, to challenge the King and the Queen and even the highest authorities. They become the personification of bravery, unpredictability & unseen creativity because of which they gain mastery in their work very fast. They often take the paths less travelled and even forge completely original paths in the wild, tailor made just for them, all by themselves which are designed in alignment to their individuality and life purpose.

Ketu, on the other hand is another shadow planet and signifies the south node, which is basically the past. The memories, connections, gifts, talents, wisdom and karma of the past lives are brought into the present life through Ketu. It is the portal through which that energy is received by the individual, whether good or bad. A lot of these **predetermined skills** and **predestined paths** of the Chosen Ones is basically ancient wisdom and inner knowing of the soul, which gets downloaded in the current life. It already exists in the blueprint of the soul and can be accessed by the expanded consciousness of the individual. As they walk on the path of their life purpose these inner knowings are unlocked slowly and the access is granted by the divine. Once they are focused and work with their north node towards their destiny, great opportunities and events unfold in their life with which they accomplish a lot.

3. THE DIVINE WALKS WITH THEM IN EVERY STEP, THEIR EVERY MOVE IS GUIDED

They follow their intuition for regular day to day activities, because they never know how the events are being planned by the universe and how the jewels of life are going to get revealed to them. Intuition is a muscle and they work on that muscle everyday to make it agile and strong. They exercise listening to the intuition, reading the energy of a room/space, analyzing energy and body language of people on a regular basis and use this guidance before making any decision and due to this their psychic gifts & intuitive power keeps getting stronger as they grow older.

4. THEY WILL INITIALLY PLAY THE ROLE OF THE BLACK SHEEP IN THEIR LIFE

They won't fit in with their surroundings in their initial years, they will be the odd ones asking all the weird questions, pointing out flaws and have hobbies that might appear strange to others. They might have unique gifts like proper communication to plants, trees and animals. Have an extended sense of compassion or display connection with the spirit at an early age. As they grow a bit older they might pick very different career paths than their community, change their faith and stay distant from their original blood family. They might stay aloof to protect themselves from various negative mindsets and lifestyles which can harm their growth trajectory, they have learnt ways to protect themselves due to facing repeated harsh circumstances in their life. They will be labelled as the black sheeps of the family initially because of these unique abilities and will be treated negatively until they fulfil their purpose.

EVENTS THAT OCCUR AS THE CHOSEN ONE STARTS BREAKING THE PATTERN

1. BLACK SHEEP BLOWING THE WHISTLE, CAUSING DISRUPTION

As the Black sheep awakens, it might happen at an early age or even at a later stage, they will start speaking out about the dysfunction that has been going on for decades, the black sheep is playing the role of a whistleblower for the rest of the family. The very next thing is a huge disruption in the family, the black sheep goes out of the family unit, it can be a society, it can be a community, it can be a place where you have grown that has been accustomed to certain kind of toxic ideas and those ideas have been picked up from previous generations. Here we are addressing dysfunctions whether it is in a family, in a community or in the society in general. The black sheep leaves the dysfunctional unit, goes out and starts a life of their own free from the patterns. They will reproduce and start a family of their own, these children born from the Chosen Ones unit will be the seed of a new healed bloodline, they will be a fresh branch of lineage coming out from the original stem after much healing from all kinds of childhood and adulthood trauma.

2. CHAOS IN THE DYSFUNCTIONAL UNIT

Meanwhile there's a lot of chaos that is going on in the family as a result of the Aftermath, people pointing fingers at each other, playing the blame game and a lot of fights within each other. As the whistle is blown, the entire family unit starting from the oldest member to the youngest generation gets disturbed and triggered. The cat is out of the bag, the secrets are out and clearly visible for everyone to see. The whistle blower starts saying everything openly about what is going on and gradually makes everyone aware of everything. This leads to insecurity within the older members of the family and they blame each other initially to clean their dirty hands. The aunt will blame the uncle, the wife will blame the husband, the older cousin will point fingers at another cousin's wife etc.

3. SHIFTING BLAME ON THE BLACK SHEEP AGAIN

Now seeing all the chaos in the family the eldest member who is consumed by the dysfunctions and makes everyone follow them will be highly stressed and will think of a game plan to shift the focus elsewhere. The eldest member now goes to the other family members and tries to brainwash them that everything the black sheep was saying is false, that it's not the truth. He asks every other member to calm down and tries to convince them to believe in this false picture that he is trying to paint to frame the Black sheep again. He tries to bring the other members to his side and tries to gang up against the black sheep. But this time although some of the loyal members do stay on their side and believe the false story, there are also some members who know that actually what the black sheep said was true. The Chosen One did actually help in opening the eyes of a few people.

4. THE CHOSEN ONE REMAINS UNBOTH-ERED

A lot of gossip, slander and false stories do circulate around the Chosen now, as the dysfunctional family still tries hard to cover up everything that got exposed. But remember the Chosen is a very strong individual and they usually can stand all alone irrespective of any amount of dirt thrown at them. They can leave the whole dysfunction and separate themselves from that destruction sometimes temporarily and most of the time permanently. In most of the cases a Chosen will leave for good but they will not leave without blowing the whistle to aid the other members.

5. OTHERS TAKING INSPIRED ACTION & FALLING OFF THE FAMILY TREE

Now the ones who became aware of the situation and didn't believe the false stories created by the elders, who saw truth in the perspective shown by the Chosen will take an inspired action. There might be a few of them, not all who will also leave the dysfunctional unit for good, maintain contact with them only from a distance and as a result fall off from the family tree. Every member that separates themselves for good from that family unit is now branching out and starting their own bloodline, with a different way of parenting their children and starting a healthier pattern which gets passed on gradually. These families are now created from a higher frequency of love, respect, equality and mutual benefit.

These ancestral patterns and generation curses are only broken by love, because love is the highest frequency in the universe, it is the frequency that we all can use to overcome anything, which is why that is the biggest reason a Chosen One is punished and picked on without a reason in their childhood. Chosen Ones are born with a very high frequency, which is the frequency of love they are able to laugh, smile at people with an open heart, their compassion makes a big impact and touches hearts of any living being instantly. They are able to love people unconditionally. That's the secret equipment the empath uses, that is an innate advantage the Chosen One has, over the other family members and anybody else.

Meanwhile the die-hards of the family system who are loyal to the authority and obey the oppression are the mates who decide to stay with the unit forever, to die with them.

6. THE NEW GENERATION WILL BE BORN INTO ABUNDANCE

As we know the Chosen One leaves the family tree after creating a disruption, moves away and starts a new healed bloodline. Now these children born of the Chosen will be the generation to experience abundance. These children are born after breaking the patterns of **lack, poverty, narcissism, low vibrational habits and**

addictions like alcohol addiction, drug addiction, gambling, adultery in marriage, early deaths, domestic violence, servant abuse etc. This generation is born into Abundance, into love, they are born into true happiness and freedom.

7. THE SPIRITUAL PERSPECTIVE - WHAT HAPPENS BEHIND THE VEIL

What is happening behind the veil? Because remember by breaking the generational cycle you are not just breaking the patterns in the physical realm but you're also breaking this whole thing in the spiritual realm. These bloodline cases are always associated with demonic and evil energies, because the dysfunctions and addictions are nothing but evil energy, evil entities manifesting as evil actions or bad *karma*. These energies have blocked those people from prospering, from developing into successful individuals, from becoming pure and living a healthy lifestyle, from rising into the higher frequencies of Love, Peace and Purpose. It's these entities who trap the weak individuals generation after generation and keep them locked in extremely low vibration. They have deprived them of the chance to be internally and spiritually fulfilled.

But now due to the brave efforts of the Chosen, the changes occur first in the spiritual realm and then start trickling down in the physical realm as well. The spiritual changes start mirroring in the 3D reality of everyone. The Chosen get their reward for doing the difficult job and opening a dam of Abundance, which is received by them and their family. It is not just an abundance of wealth and money or opportunities at work, but it is an abundance of many things. Of divine favor, of intuition, of inner peace, life purpose, wisdom, love, emotional satisfaction and a drive to pass on the wisdom to others worldwide who need to break similar patterns in their own bloodline.

Not forgetting to mention that the Chosen also gets promoted in their spiritual rank for showing courage in difficult times, for not giving up in the darkest and weakest moments, for having faith in the divine no matter what showed up, for being able to use discernment while making critical decisions and relentlessly working towards their mission everyday. And with the increase in their rank, there is an increase in their spiritual privileges too, which is solid divine protection, access to rare portals, heightened psychic gifts, synchronistic events, divinely guided opportunities, heightened manifestation powers and much more.

8. DOWNFALL OR DEMISE OF THE ORIGINAL CURSE BEARER

The original curse bearer generation who are responsible for passing the curse to their offsprings will see a gradual downfall. Their health will start to deteriorate intensely and they might get diagnosed with life threatening diseases. As the cycle was interrupted and there is an abrupt discontinuation of the cycle, all the negative energy, the curse and dysfunctional mindset now remains stagnant with the curse bearer. It is unable to flow to anyone. In the spiritual realm the evil entities who were working through this person sort of devour this person now as a part of punishment for not being able to continue passing down the dysfunction.

When you are working with negative entities your entire life, letting these entities take control of you, letting them use your vessel for conducting evil *karma*, it is like making a deal with the devil, selling your soul to the devil for gains that the devil promised you but is ultimately an illusion. The devil is a lower vibrational entity, it is not GOD, it is the opposite in every way. It doesn't give you what it has promised, even if you worship it. It lures you with all kinds of temptations, fake promises and illusions. It just uses you for its wishes and then discards you once you have played your part. And when you have failed to do your task it will make you pay the price yourself. It will devour you, your soul, your body. You won't have anything left. A lot of people do not understand that, they get tempted easily into doing the lower vibrational actions for instant growth, instant fame and power. Sometimes they even get it but it doesnt stay, it comes as a flash and leaves. Because it isn't real after all, it's just an illusion. Then the person gets frustrated and ends up doing more wrong deeds to get some more of it, it becomes like a bait, thinking this time it will stay. But in that process they accumulate heaps of bad *karma* and fall into the trap of a dysfunctioning cycle where they don't gain anything anyway but just keep feeding the devil with their soul.

The original curse bearer hence gets destroyed by the devil himself as they are having to pay an alternate price. They even start looking devilish, their bodies start rotting, their organs start failing. The negative energy in their body and mind starts manifesting as cancer or some form of life ending disease. Although their minds are aware of what is happening, they are nearing their end and at this point they are aware of the repercussions of their doings, of what is to come of their evil *karma*. Their whole life starts to play in their head like a movie and they keep watching it in silence not saying much to anyone.

9. DEATH OF THE CURSE BEARER MOSTLY OCCURS AFTER THE CHOSEN ONE BREAKS THE CYCLE

Now there is a slight criteria that should be ideally fulfilled so that you can make sure that the dysfunction ends with the death of the curse bearer. If the person dies without anybody waking up in that family that cycle will now be passed on to the children of the

Chosen Ones generation and the cycle will continue. But when the Chosen has awakened and the cycle has been disrupted even before starting a family and having children, you can make sure that the pattern will end. Now when the Curse bearer dies due to ill health or old age the dysfunction dies with them. This is when the cycle ends at the physical level and also in the spiritual realm.

10. THE BLACK SHEEP BECOMES THE G.O.A.T

Now the Chosen One is considered '**The G.O.A.T, The Greatest Of All Times'**, in their bloodline, they will be remembered by the past Ancestors, present and all the future generations as the curse breaker and bringer of Generational Abundance. They will be saluted for being the Black sheep, for having gone through a very difficult life, for having the courage to stand up against the authorities boldly, for being the person who was the most hated but ultimately completed their life purpose and spiritual mission successfully.

FOR THE FAMILY SCAPEGOATS, LEAVING A DYSFUNCTIONAL FAMILY

1. DO NOT LOOK BACK

When you leave these kinds of dysfunctional family units do not look behind because when you look back you're not going to like what you see. As a person who's escaping narcissistic abuse and you have escaped well from your family you have got to know that the narcissistic parent is leaving faster than you expected. After the narcissistic injury they are going to go through a total decomposition process so they're going to start decaying. The reason why they're going to decompose is because you have unplugged their energy batteries, you have unplugged their supply cables, their supply chains, it has switched off their energy batteries and they do not know how to create their own fuel. They only take it from others. You were their supply remember, they were feeding off you all these years and now you have left them there without supply, without fuel. They do not have any fuel batteries left and hence you will experience their collapse. You might hear it from people, they may come around and tell you that they have seen your father, your mother, they're looking like they're going to die, they are looking very sick and depleted. They're looking like the walking dead, it is painful to watch because you considered them your family all your life.

So for us, the people who have done it, we know what it looks like. It's very painful to look at them, because you are still an Empath and you still feel Empathy and compassion for them even after everything. And this trait of yours can bring everything back crumbling down again, ruining everything that you have worked so hard on so far. So when you leave such family units you have got to make sure of one thing that is you **DON'T LOOK BACK**. Keep on working on yourself and don't look back because these curse bearers first of all after they go through the narcissistic injury they are going to start craving for fuel, for supply and they're going to start biting off other members that are living with them. And most of the time those family members are not used to that kind of abuse, so they won't give in easily. And then the curse bearers start scavenging and looking for alternative sources for fuel. And in some cases when there's nobody around, where most of the potential family members have left and are carrying on with their life, the curse bearers wont stay alive for very long, they finally give up and die. We have heard many cases where the curse bearers have died in just a couple of months after the Black sheep has left the unit.

Now this is a very crucial point in your curse breaking journey which no one talks about. The moment you unplug the curse bearers from your fuel systems their health will deteriorate and you will realise that in a very short period of time, they are appearing like Zombies and are soon going to hit the grave. You will start hearing all kinds of news from other distant family members that they have been hospitalised, that they were on the verge of dying and somehow survived, that their organs are failing etc etc. You are going to hear many things that you don't even want to hear, so do not be surprised when those same people reach out to you in sly ways, try to emotionally manipulate you and try very hard to suck you back into the family. They will act very ambitious and they actually perceive that they can suck you back into the rut to scapegoat you like usual. It is very difficult to replace a scapegoat, you are a scapegoat for a reason. They won't be able to use and blame any other person that easily like they did with you. Behind closed doors they accept that your presence in that family is very important for their energetic survival even if they did not want to acknowledge that to you ever. You were and you are very important in that family which is why they will send out many messages through relatives to hook you and pull you back into the family, saying 'your mommy is missing you, your daddy is very sick and wants to see you', 'let's have dinner together on Thanksgiving, let's enjoy this Christmas together' etc. It sounds harsh and anyone might think of you as an **ungrateful heartless monster** for deciding to not meet your sick parents but they do not know what your life purpose is, they don't know what you have gone through, how much you have suffered by the hands of those same sick people, what is your life story, how you are breaking a curse and how you are the Chosen who is handpicked for this work. They do not know anything but they will come around as messengers and judge you, compare their stories with you. So please, do not listen to anyone who comes to you advising you to re enter the dysfunctional unit or give them your energy in any way. When the family unit has no more scapegoats and is desperate it is a very dangerous phase of blame game, emotional manipulation and judgements. In no way, shape or form are you supposed to look back and return.

2. THE HERMIT MODE - LONELY & EMOTIONAL

You are starting a new life and in the first few months or even for a couple of years initially for some, you're going to struggle a bit. You will feel lonely, the feeling of being by yourself will be very intense. You would have never felt so alone like this phase. Most people will be stripped out of your life, friends, partners no one will be left. You will want to crawl back into old friendships at times out of desperation, on certain weekends, on certain holidays, birthdays, special festivals because you will want to talk and celebrate at least with someone. But most of the time you won't be able to connect with anyone, either they won't pick up, they won't be able to reach you or meet you or it just won't align. Those are the testing times, the universe testing your strength and dedication. Can you stay strong and follow through without falling back on the past energies? Can you push through, turn your pain into power and keep moving ahead or are you going to feel needy and helpless and give up on your journey. How much faith do you have in the Most High? Do you believe in your journey of being a Chosen One? Are you going to waste all that you went through all your life just because you are alone now? Most of these people are from your past, from the cycles that you have left behind which is why the divine won't let you connect with them back. You will be left alone even on your birthdays, new years and important days of the year. It will hurt a lot, you will wonder why isn't it over, why arent your tough days coming to an end. You will question your journey many times over and over again, you will doubt if you are on the right path, during your weakest moments but you will have to come back and ground yourself wherever you are each and every time.

During this phase of mine, when I had finally hit the last nail with family and had completely cut off everything in my life, I was so lonely that the dark energy would come to me many times making me feel worthless and lost at times, to a point when I would even feel the suicidal energy in my head. Those very dark self harm thoughts would arise and I would just observe them. I would be very sure that this energy is not mine, it's coming from elsewhere, coming from outside me, being sent to me or projected at me, those are not my thoughts at all, they cannot be, because I know I cannot perform self harm on myself ever. I have never done any mild form of physical self harm even on my worst days and I know how much I love myself, I can never hit that low. So I would feel the energy, hear the thoughts in my head and quickly release it saying it's not mine. It's very important to discern your own thoughts and feelings and take the right action in those fragile moments, dear Chosen.

You might shed a lot of tears looking at your situation, looking at yourself in the mirror. But you will gradually come to understand that a huge phase of your life is over and a completely new phase, a new story has begun which requires you to start from scratch and that needs you to be patient. It needs you to wait and watch, have faith and let the days roll without needing to connect with anyone from the past. You are supposed to make use of this lone phase and find yourself. The Chosen Ones at this point go deep within themselves because of the amount of time they get on their own. There are no distractions, no unnecessary people with their mindless conversations, no going out too much etc. Your lifestyle will change drastically at this point. You might cut out all toxic habits, like drinking, smoking, eating non veg and wasting time in any other way. You also might quit your regular jobs and do something on your own which makes you happy and lets you express yourself better. In that process you will end up cutting a lot of noise in the form of people, places and information which does not resonate with your new life. You will struggle with your emotions initially yes but this is the period when you will learn and master how to manage your emotions.

3. YOU ARE NOT ALONE, THE SPIRIT REALM IS ALWAYS AROUND YOU

In this particular Lone Wolf or Hermit phase we do feel lonely because we are so used to having people around us, having humans around us in general. But gradually as we ground ourselves and observe our environment we realize that we are not alone. We were never alone in the first place ever and we very definitely are not alone now. The whole point of isolation and going Hermit mode after the whole family fiasco is to make you more aware of the existence of your spiritual team. You know that only when you shut out some of your senses the other senses that we don't use get more awakened and become stronger, right. A lot of people who pursue spirituality of a serious and advanced level enter such phases and journeys where they remain secluded from society and live in caves, in darkness with minimal resources. They only spend their time retrospecting and connecting with ethereal energies which becomes possible as they shut out some of their other basic senses. It activates their mind, intuition and opens up certain higher chakras which can access various cosmic portals and communicate with supernatural, universal and ethereal entities. Even the practice of *'Vipasna'* which has become quite popular amongst the youth even in the cities is about shutting out some amount of communication, physical senses and external stimulation to detox our vessel and find a way to connect with ourselves internally. Practising *'Vipasna'* for 10 days can be very beneficial to our mind and body in terms of spiritual growth and internal journey. A Chosen basically goes through these forced Vipasna states which are designed by the divine and are conducted during the divine timing. Because we have less control over our spiritual journey, the duration of these phases and level of difficulty we are meant to surrender ourselves to it and go with the flow. Just consider all the situations thrown at us as a learning ground where we are getting trained for our next phases.

I have always spoken about these phases as our **'PRIVILEGED PHASES'**. Isolation is not a punishment but a huge privilege. As you will be spending all of your energy on yourself and on nobody else. The life force, the precious *prana* which gets used for doing every little task throughout the day, which also determines how you look, how you talk and walk and think is all available exclusively to you. Can you understand what kind of a privilege that is? Most of us can't because we never looked at it from that perspective. No one has told us that, no one ever has thought of it like that. But since childhood we are only told to use our life force for others and ourselves and give it away like it's just there always. But we are never told that it's limited, it's not going to last forever. It's going to last till the time you are alive and overusing or over giving it will drain you and lower the quality of your everyday life. What is the point of living a low quality life where you are tired all the time, you don't have energy left for yourself at the end of the day, you are stressed and miserable and are never able to do what you desire because of bad management of your energy. The huge chunk of energy that you started with in the morning got all used up by others. You are draining your precious life force and not able to think right, do your important tasks right and live up to any of your dreams right. The ideal way is to always have enough energy left even at the end of the day and never being in the energy of burn out. Because we are here to live and experience every moment of every day with curiosity and zest. Even when we are going to sleep and entering the dream state it requires a good amount of energy to astral travel, to receive information, enter many other astral dimensions and work with them. Dreams are nothing but alternate zones of consciousness which the mind accesses when the body comes to a complete recess. By the time our consciousness comes back and enters our vessel we need to have enough energy left in order to wake up fresh in the morning the next day. A lot of times we wake up very tired even after a full night's sleep because your body was resting but your mind was very active all throughout. But when you are able to preserve a lot of energy in the day for weeks and months you will have a reservoir of life force in your body which won't burn out easily. Which is why we need to look at these 'HERMIT' phases as advantages we have over others. Very few people are chosen to live such lives and experience such modes of rejuvenation and self exploration.

4. FINDING CLOSURE THROUGH THE DIVINE

• CLEARING

Don't confuse this phase with the original branching off and breaking out of the family phase. This is the next phase of shedding all the extra bulky non essential energy in your life. This period has been given to the Chosen for initiating many things in their life. We all know that new energy, opportunities and the right aligned people will be able to enter your reality only when we let go of the old energy, you have to make space basically just like spring cleaning or a clearance sale to usher in high frequency divine potent energy which will manifest as people, opportunities, wealth and contentment. A thorough cleansing of your life takes place during this time. I don't remember if I mentioned it earlier but a regular job, a 9 to 5, or some monotonous donkey work which is holding you back will be cleared from your energy field and mostly be replaced by something connected to your passion and purpose even if in a very humble way without making much profit initially. Along with the job, the toxic energy of your colleagues, co workers, clients, bosses, the spaces, stress and anxiety related to that job will also be cleared. If not replaced you will be nudged big time to look within and find what you are supposed to do. Constant reminders such as visions, angel numbers, dreams, songs, pop ups from Youtube, memes etc will follow you around to keep pushing you towards your alignment. Along with co workers, even a complete detox of friends and family will also initiate which is confusing and deeply painful because we can only count on them but there might be many instances where they end up showing their true self and reveal their true intention towards you. There will come a point when putting on a show, wearing a mask will become very difficult, they won't be able to act anymore, their envy and hate towards you will seem uncontainable. Which is why once the divine shows you their true self we must not reason with it further. There will be no gain by repeating those cycles a few more times, it will only get more ugly, more shocking and you will not learn anything new. It will tire you out and waste your time. So once these cycles are divinely ended we must go with the flow. They will come around when they no longer see you as a threat when they reach a closer frequency as yours and until then you must respect your own energy levels.

• SHADOW WORK - 'HURT PEOPLE, HURT PEOPLE'

This phase will also initiate the deep shadow work that one needs to do. Am sure we all have heard of 'Shadow work', 'inner work', 'deep soul work' and why we need to do that. But we end up thinking that doing a couple of sessions here and there is going to be enough. We do feel relieved, we feel like we have cleared a lot at that moment which is why we think it is enough, but not my dear. There is so much that we need to clear we cannot even imagine, which is why this deep shadow work initiates upon us during this phase. This kind of deep retrospection, deep inner dialogue by going completely within, understanding ourselves at the soul level which can unlock secrets of our past, present and future is possible only during a medium to long term isolation phase. Like we spoke about earlier, because of all the thorough clearance and creating space, now you will be inviting divine pure higher self energy into your life which will know exactly what you need at this time. It will gradually reveal many secrets about you, about where you came from, why you are here, what other information you need to know at this point, what are going to be the next steps and how you are going to prepare for it. All sorts of alignments will start happening right in front of your eyes which will seem miraculous to you initially, yes it is a miracle in a way which you will also need to have gratitude for.

HOW EXACTLY IS 'SHADOW WORK' DONE?

The more shadow work you do, the more negative energy you will release from your entire soul and being. Negative energy which is pent up in your entire being from all kinds of trauma from childhood, school, relationships, parents, bullying, marriage, jobs, co workers, online harassment, physical abuse, accidents, evil eye, black magic, generational curses etc etc. We are not even aware of how much we are burdened by the baggage of all these events and its pent up stored energy. We carry all this baggage everyday and go about our life. We feel heavy, anxious, sad and damaged but we don't do anything about it. We still go on with our lives that way, but this deep shadow work, inner healing work will remove all of that. Now imagine if you need to remove all that negative energy stored in your being from so many years, like a few decades it is going to take some time, right? It is not going to go away in a blink of an eye, in a couple of sessions with a therapist, a few ayahuasca healing sessions, a few months of journaling, or a little bit of yoga, no. It is not going to go away so easily. After you do a couple of healing sessions you feel better but pretty soon like the next month something happens that triggers your trauma again. It makes you act out of character, reminds you of what was done to you earlier, you feel all the pain, anger and hate all over again. You may burst out in tears or end up shouting at someone hurting them badly. This shows that the pent up hurtful emotions are still there, remember 'Hurt people, hurt people'. Now every time you get triggered know that it's the divine signal to heal that section, everything related to that emotion, that event. You will have to get on a mission to understand what exactly was triggering you, which is that event that led to that, what happened in that event, who were those people involved, what did they say or do, go to the core of it. And then work on those emotions one by one, feel the pain, cry, shed those tears as long as they are coming out, understand that it was part of your destiny to go through that event and recover, understand that it happened for a reason, nothing in your life is a coincidence. And now that it has passed you can't change it, you cannot reverse time, you can only let it go once and for all. Doing these 'let go' rituals work well on a full moon portal. But you will see that it might resurface again, these emotions are stored deep in our flesh, blood and bone, they keep popping up back in the form of mental images, emotional memories and attachments. Attachments can be very negative and toxic at times, which are difficult to release just because we don't see these attachments for what they are at present, but how comfortable it felt in the past and the possibility of how good it can be in the future. We fail to look at how they are in the 'now' moment which actually is most important for your healing. Which is why we will need to keep working on the triggers over and over again as many times as they appear, as many times as it is required. After you have been in this phase for a couple of years you will gradually have the heart to **forgive** each and everyone who wronged you. You will be able to forgive even the darkest crimes and set free. It is very important to do that, for yourself alone. Remember holding onto hate and anger will keep building the negative energy in your body which ultimately will manifest into life threatening diseases. Forgiving those people is not for them, it's for you, really. It is for you, so you can set free and fly away like a bird who has never seen pain. To reverse many things, to feel like a newborn, to conquer your own emotions and give yourself a second chance. This solitude phase is ideal and designed to stay in your life for all of that consistent shadow work as long as it needs for you to relieve all that baggage and feel free, light and authentically happy from within.

• ADAPTING TO THIS LIFESTYLE AND OWNING IT

This phase can go on from a few years to even a decade depending on what kind of past you have had, what is your future and if you are healing traumas of not just yourself but your entire bloodline. Gradually you will adapt to this lifestyle, you will start seeing the pros and understand that the cons were mostly toxic familiarities of the past and the absence of peace. Soon you will start enjoying this new life and understand that the divine has given you what you needed and not what you wanted. Because they know what is best for you, for real. Soon, you will start seeing the blessings of being by yourself, the divine synchronicities will surprise you, the silence won't be deafening anymore, you will recognize it as peace. We are not used to so much peace actually, which is why we are scared of it. But you will be introduced to a different life which you will appreciate ultimately. You might be even moved from the city to the countryside to get you close to nature, to open up your senses, you might be shifted across the state or country in order to find proper isolation. And you will be grateful for it. With time passing you will realize living by yourself is a privilege and not any form of compromise or sacrifice, which was never experienced before and no man had ever spoken about it being safe or normal. They only scared us by saying all humans are social beings so we must never leave our pride and community no matter how much it misunderstands us and holds us back. Isolation is a part of a Chosen One's journey, which is unavoidable. The more we run away from it the more we will struggle. It's only best to surrender to the divine's plan and go on a deep spiritual healing journey. It is only normal when you are a Chosen One.

• FINDING THE DIVINE WITHIN YOU

After you have found comfort with your new lifestyle and striking a balance with what you have and what you don't, you will come across many revelations about yourself, about the angelic realm, about how the universe is constantly working with you etc. You might be informed about why you were born under the influence of certain planets and stars, which constellations align with your purpose, how your birth chart looks, which planets in your birth chart need to be worked on so that you can align with your life purpose and reach your goals faster. If you were confused as to why certain kinds of relationships aren't working out or why you had to face betrayal in some areas of your life, those doubts also get cleared with the revelation of your birth chart. Certain information regarding your past life which are important and very relevant to the present life might emerge, gifts that you have carried into this reincarnation from the past lives, gifts and talents that are maybe hidden at this point which you are unaware of but need your realisation and a push from your end so that they get exposed as they are a part of your present personality and life mission. You might get pushed to work with certain deities, which necessarily don't belong to your faith or country, you might be encouraged to conduct rituals in respect to those deities and energies, because you need their blessings, protection and power at this phase of your life. Your entire life will start shifting at this point, your morning rituals, sleeping patterns can change, the schedule of the day might get altered altogether, your daily priorities will change, you will be encouraged to change your diet into a healthy one, you might turn into a vegetarian who eats once a day etc. And because you will understand everything that you are going through is because of your past karma and nothing else, you will try to clear more of your bad karma by doing good deeds like donations, feeding the poor, feeding animals, having a prayer lifestyle etc. All of these revelations, awakenings and regular spiritual practices will raise your default vibration by many notches. You will be vibrating at a much higher frequency now and you will reach a state of great mental clarity. Your emotions will no longer control you and you won't be hurt by others easily. Your tolerance bar will also raise, your aura will be impenetrable making you very strong. You will enjoy this whole 'living off the grid' lifestyle where you feel so powerful that you no longer care about how people see you. This intense healing work and divination will allow the divine energies to come through and work with you. You will feel the **divine within you, their energy living in your house and their protective bubble all**

around you. And once you genuinely feel that for sometime you won't want to give it up for anything in this world.

You will feel your ancestors, your spirit guides, angels and ascended masters working with you at every step. They have been protecting and watching you since you were born anyway but now the difference is that you are aware of it. And this awareness makes the energy more powerful, it's like you give complete permission to them to remove obstacles from your way, you walk hand in hand with them and co-create with your angels on a regular level. Because your intuition has heightened you can receive downloads easily and follow the guidance of your angels to move on the right path, find the next steps and do your tasks with ease. You will be seeing yourself give birth to a brand new self, a divine rebirth will take place right in front of your eyes and everyone. Your highest and best version will emerge, of course there is no end to bettering and enhancing yourself but this will definitely feel like a divine glow up that was long awaited and had arrived in the perfect timing. This glow up is happening at many levels, physical, emotional, mental, intellectual and spiritual. It is a glow up from all aspects because the intense healing work has opened all your chakras/energy centres. All the blockages are removed from the energy centres and your life force is flowing peacefully from one chakra to another. Along with easy reception of divine energy through your open crown and soul star chakra which connects with the astral planes. It is a beautiful state of balance where you feel the duality of life. **You will feel powerful yet peaceful, beautiful yet humble, infinite yet minute and you will look at yourself as everything yet nothing.** You will feel like you are a part of something so huge you never knew existed, you will feel very abundant. This 'new you' will shock you, exasperate you, fill you with joy because of how much you have conquered and overcome and make you weep at the same time while you realise that life is still so fragile that anything can happen at anytime and everything and every living being you love so dearly can evaporate at any moment. Now that life looks so beautiful to you and all the struggles you have passed you will realise that you have very limited time on earth, a 100 years of a human's life is actually very little time in cosmic comparison. Our existence is like a speck of dust wiped away in one blow when you look at it from the cosmos. We came, barely sat down and understood the game and it's already time to leave. You will realise how much time we have already wasted by dwelling in the negative energy, all the insignificant conversations, egos, wrong people, places and things that didn't allow you to rise up to this 'new you'. You will see how profound your life actually is if you allow it. This 'new you' which you didn't know existed, no one knew existed beneath the layers, beneath all the trauma, will show you a different side to the world. Your high frequency will be the portal to enter the abundant side of the world, always remember as your frequency keeps rising you will keep having newer glow ups and will be able to enter new portals leading to a new reality around you.

Now that you have risen so high, you know your real value, you know who you are and you are continuously raising the bar, you will no longer be asking for the same price. What you are now supposed to receive in exchange of your energy is very high. It will become clear to you in time about how you are supposed to price your energy because your energy is not regular anymore, it is celestial and divine. You are not supposed to settle for anything less than what matches your current frequency. It applies to every-thing, people, places, opportunities, jobs, looks, conversations and mindsets. Because if you start settling for less, you are going to ruin your current frequency, it will start dropping to the level of the old toxic environments. You will also be disrespecting all your angels, guides and ancestors, their hard work behind creating you and most importantly you will be letting down yourself. Things that you have outgrown must be left behind and with no remorse or guilt because at this point you must realise, it's going to be **'YOU and the DIVINE'** in collaboration for the rest of your life. The ones you have left behind will do fine without you, God and their spirit guides will look after them and they have their own journeys to follow and healing to do. You cannot take everyone with you into your new life, you must walk your path now looking forward only. Once you have understood and *innerstood* it from within, you will be able to find closure, even if you are not in communication with some individuals since the breaking off. You will find closure even if it's in silence, because you know that you and them have played your parts in each other's life, and no one can blame you for anything.

• SHOWING COMPASSION FROM A DISTANCE

Now, we are in that stage of finding closure on our own with the help of the divine, silent closure in your heart that will bring peace to you, no longer making you feel miserable or trigger you. The triggers might reappear time and time again but every time you get triggered you will have to practise forgiveness and work towards ending the cycle. Remember every time you feel anger towards them you are only fueling it and not letting the cycle end. But when you are able to forgive and move on, you are not just helping yourself but also freeing the other person from this karmic cycle. Because you are the bigger person here, as the **Chosen One**, who has chosen to do the healing work for the entire bloodline. Your ancestors, the previous generations and future generations will be grateful to you for having the courage and compassion to forgive all of them and helping them move on from that toxic karmic cycle and grow. Never forget that you are here to heal your bloodline, you are the strongest contender in your entire bloodline chosen for this monumental work and being forgiving and compassionate is a must have characteristic of a true Chosen One. You must find closure from each and every karmic cycle in time, whether it's family, friends, co workers, partners, children or spouse etc.

Now if I have to speak about myself I had been writing this book for 2 years and even while writing this book, I got triggered many times. While writing my stories I had to relive each one, feel the emotions, go through the events turn by turn while putting in the details and the negative emotions kept flowing into my head. It did make me furious, many times, where I even kept mumbling things that I would say to them if they were in front of me. I would keep thinking of what I should have said when those events had happened in the past, it would ruin a couple of hours of mine and sometimes I would wake up in that same mad energy, feeling stuck. But soon I would realize that I was only fueling that toxic connection by doing all of this. And I would try very hard to come out of that energy to complete my tasks, to get up, show up and start my day. This would tell me that I have so much more healing to do. These triggers are basically your guides, your teachers, you come to know what you need to work on more. I would follow that guidance and do more shadow work, go deep into my soul, my mind and my flesh to heal as much as I can.

Now some people out of the entire lot that you have let go and cut chords might need your compassion, like your parents. Like I have said before, we can replace most toxic and narcissistic connections like friends, partners and colleagues but you can't replace parents even if they are toxic. You just get a couple of them in your life and you can't change them even if you want, which is why it's the most difficult connection when gone wrong. As you are going through the healing work and finding closure gradually the degree of hate, anger and revenge has gotten smaller and smaller. At some point you will be able to forgive them completely and find closure deep in your heart, and you will become strong and pure enough to show compassion from a distance. Mind it, I am still saying from a distance, energetically you can send them healing thoughts, prayers and wish them well. You are no longer feeling vengeful, getting triggered too badly or thinking of what you should have told them to set them right. You are in a much higher vibration now where you have let that past go like it was in your past life, you are no longer attached to it emotionally. Even when you speak of it or write about it you are much more peaceful and narrate it like a story with the details but don't go off track into your negative emotions. You are very balanced and healed. Like I have mentioned before, Chosen Ones once you have stepped out of the trauma tree don't look back, don't go back. Yes you can show compassion but only from a distance, don't think you are too powerful now that you can go back and change them or heal them without getting affected yourself. It is very important to respect the amount of healing work you have done on yourself, of course once you have come this far and done all this work you will know it yourself, you wont need a reminder of how precious your state of being is and how much you need to protect it. Don't forget, the generational curses are still active at your family's original place, and all those people, places, situations and energies you left behind are still looking at you trying to attach them to you at any given chance. So you must tread carefully at all times. All your healing and ascension can crumble back and come down crashing if you are not careful and let old energies come too close to you at this point. Even saints and highly spiritual people who have attained much higher states of ascension are very strict with their day to day activities. What they eat, whom they meet, how much energy they spend in each interaction, the decision to even shake hands or not, to allow somebody to touch them or not, what they wear, where they rest, what they listen to and watch, everything is planned and thought through with a least degree of leniency. Because they know, everything is a game of energy, just because someone is vibrating at a higher frequency today doesn't mean it cannot be messed with. If even the purest saints hang out with criminals they will mess with their state of being, maybe the criminals will change a bit too but why will the saints risk all the work they put in. Our life is a game of energetic existence, it's just about which frequency we choose to exist in, our life starts turning into that, and it is a lifelong choice. Which is why we suggest Chosen Ones to give compassion from a distance to everyone they have left behind, and maintain the high vibe all throughout their life and only aim for even higher states of ascension.

• THINGS I DID TO DO DEEP INNER HEALING WORK

Journaling, Praying, Affirmations on how I wanted to see myself in the future, working with portals to jump Timelines, Mirror work, Taking care of my physical vessel through exercise and un-conditional pampering, Connecting to deities, Chanting specific mantras for specific results, Formal soul retrieval sessions on new moons with herbs for 4 years, Formal 'cord cutting' and 'letting go' sessions on full moons for 5 years, joining spiritual communities on Youtube where we did mass chants and mass affirmations to-gether, (which is very beneficial because when 1000 people chant together at one time, each person receives the effects of a 1000 times), turning complete vegetarian (no egg also), identifying all karmic connections and letting them go one by one with divine timing, not looking back and falling back into any karmic bonds or patterns of the past, having genuine strong boundaries and not letting people, places and situations to crawl back into my current timeline, connecting to nature, moving to a countryside neigh-bourhood, staying single and celebate to not invite other energies and their traumas into my life and my vessel, not feeling desperate and staying just in my energy until I actually connect with anyone at my frequency. When you do such hard work at getting rid of your traumas, you would never want to invite another person's baggage into your energy, and getting intimate is just like plugging a USB infected with viruses into a laptop. Improving my overall social habits, cutting out alcohol from my life, using my time in the most productive and peaceful way, taking exciting classes of hobbies that I have always wanted to take but couldn't make time for earlier, preferring to enjoy my solo energy more than being in unnecessary crowds or people, donating sufficiently to the poor and animals to clear out bad karma, conducting energy healing sessions from a distance on people who I had hurt in my earlier life (they were not aware of it), like for example if I had hurt them emotionally and I know that there heart is blocked to give and receive any form of love I would work on healing their heart chakra and try opening it again. I started working closely with my angels, spirit guides, my esteemed ancestors and ascended masters whose guidance I never ignored. Gradually a straight channel of communication opened up with them and I could converse with them directly, there were way too many synchronicities and aligned events happening for me to take it lightly, it was getting extremely obvious. I started bonding with my ancestor spirits more after conducting rituals for weeks during *'Pitru Paksha'* period which is the annual holy Ancestral fortnight in Hinduism when our Ancestors descend on the earthly realm from their plane and we mourn, worship and make offerings to the needy in honor and remembrance of them.

- ## WHAT IS THE REAL PRIZE FOR ALL THIS WORK?

Additionally, I learnt every form of divination to connect with the highest source from where we receive our life force. I learnt how to read tarot cards, get oracle readings, various sciences of numerology, astrology, palm reading, face reading, vastu shastra (science of space), colour therapy etc. And applied most of those learnings in my life. There is no point in joining courses and learning so many things if you aren't able to apply them practically in your life and benefit yourself. I did apply all those learnings in my life for years to see if it makes any difference and man! Yes, it does make a hell of a difference. Only thing is we will need to have patience and complete faith and not want to see results overnight. Everything takes time, just like when you sow a seed you don't see a plant and flowers overnight. You water it everyday and nurture it with sunlight and manure regularly, you show it care and concern everyday and then finally the seed germinates and you see a sapling after a few weeks. We are just like that living seed, but we need more nurturing and care in more ways, physically, emotionally, mentally and spiritually, because we are much more complicated living beings than a seed. You can understand that it would be foolish of anyone to expect miraculous healing and spiritual results overnight. And initially most people when they start, it begins with these desperate goals to get all of those miraculous results of manifesting financial abundance, ethereal beauty, attracting true love or a soul mate, become a celebrity millionaire etc but finally when you are through the process with a good number of years your entire perspective changes. You don't want those things so desperately anymore, you rise up above all of that. You become less forceful with the universe, you become very grateful with what you already have. You get this new attitude saying 'If I get my wishes it's fine, and even if I don't it's ok'. You are no longer selfish or greedy. You must be wondering what happened, what was the whole point of doing all of this then. After walking this path for several years you become so close to God and your higher self that your eyes open up to a new perspective, a new way of living, a new way of thinking. You finally understand that this pure connection that you were able to build with the divine, this new found relationship with God is the **'Ultimate Goal'**. This rare and most unconditional form of love which is the highest form of love is the ultimate fruit of all the sadhana that we have been doing. Which a person won't understand unless he experiences it himself. It cannot be explained in words, maybe it can be painted with colors or composed in music. But it is a state of being, it is a feeling and a certain frequency which is experienced and needs to be maintained. It is a certain priceless key to access the universe and its wonders and the key needs to be kept safe or it can be lost. There are all kinds of people here, some dont know about this key at all who are asleep, some are aware of this key who are sort of spiritual, a lot of people want access to this key who are good and bad both, but not everyone is chosen to receive this key, not everyone is meant to have this key even if they are spiritually powerful. Because it is about your unique relationship with God, it is about having a pure heart which has worked so hard and has been so obedient without a question that it has lost all of the greed and hunger of power in the process. This heart has gotten purified by the fire of the heavens, it has been tested time and time again, over and over again before it could prove its loyalty and its worth to possess the key. But my dear Chosen you are handpicked for this privilege, God wants to give you the keys to the universe so that you can fulfil your life purpose and live a wonderful life, become the masterpiece that God wants to show to the world, who has risen from the ashes and turned into the most favored God's golden child. And as a Chosen you are supposed to just follow the path shown to you through your intuition with a pure heart, of course you will have to stand the test of time, you will have to sacrifice many things, get purified by fire and prove your worthiness too like everyone else. But you have a pure heart embedded in you and you are born with your destiny already which is why the journey becomes a lot easier and less confusing for you than the rest.

I had many mentors online whose courses I took to better myself, to learn about business, book writing and publishing, various kinds of manifestations, aura reading, energy healing, how to attract abundance etc etc. I had subscriptions to many life coaches which is very essential, basically investing in yourself and your growth. And finally understanding my birth chart in detail to get better insight on my past life, to dissect my innate gifts, powers, childhood, relationships, family and my life purpose, yes your birth chart can reveal a lot to you about yourself and I want to go for past life regression soon. After all of this I definitely feel like a different person, a newborn with a different vessel and a complete soul, who has retrieved her lost soul fragments back. My energy had changed so much that I couldn't resonate with the old me anymore, I couldn't believe I was that person ever, a lot of people from my past do not recognize me, do not know how to approach me or how to treat me, because remember when your energy changes you are going to look different too. You are having multiple glow ups, one after the other and people around you are baffled with your energy upgrades as you are only aiming for higher states of ascension while maintaining a balanced high frequency everyday by default.

• FINDING YOUR PURPOSE AND GIVING IT YOUR ALL

You must be thinking why do we need to stay in the high vibe for the rest of our lives. Why can't we be like other regular people doing low vibe things? Or you must be wondering what is the point of doing all of this? What is the next stage as a Chosen One? Here is where we come to our next stage, knowing ourselves to the best we can, doing all of this healing work so that we find our life purpose and fulfill it.

We had to give up everything that was holding us back, raise ourselves to the highest frequency, transform ourselves to the best version and so much more not to just live like everyone else or to benefit ourselves but to fulfill our purpose which is much bigger than us. All of that shadow work, inner work is done so that we peel our real selves out and along with it find our most authentic talents, gifts and powers which were hidden inside. Some of us aren't aware of and some of us are aware of but we weren't confident enough to pursue. We were scared of this world, of how we were going to be perceived, of how we will be judged if we fail etc etc. But all of this healing and isolation has instilled deep faith within us. The highly unbreakable, unshakable faith in ourselves and the divine because of whom we have survived everything entirely on our own. This whole phase has taken us above the 3D programming, above all the social fear, matrix traps and unspoken social obligations. We are able to see everything clearly about what is actually needed and good for us and what is not. When you are inside the matrix you cannot perceive anything else but that because you are still operating from within the rules and dos and don'ts of the matrix. But once you have stepped out of it for a long while you can clearly spot what is absolutely discardable, what you can completely live without. What is coming in the way of your life purpose, what is limiting the practice of your gifts, talents and special abilities, what is tolerable according to you and what are those few things that you need, that are good for you and will accelerate the growth of your divine work and existence. Accordingly you can make your lifestyle choices and carry on with your life. This whole phase of your life, the deep shadow work and isolation is going to make you very wise, much wiser than people in your age group. It is going to empower you to another level with divine strength, confidence, intuition and unlocking the inner fire of passion.

This passion now needs to get channelled into your life purpose. Once you have figured out what it is, there is no stoppin you. You will be doing that everyday with all your heart. The universe will walk with you helping you manifest all the right people and opportunities to make it happen. Of course the negative energies of the dark side will still come at you and try to stop you from fulfilling your tasks with all kinds of roadblocks and temptations but you are unfuckwithable at this stage. You can no longer be manipulated, drained, delayed, taken advantage of or tempted. You have seen all of that many times before and have learnt all the lessons very well, which is why at this stage post shadow work and isolation you can spot betrayal from a mile away. Your heart has toughened so much that it doesn't break easily anymore. You can sniff the Judas out, even before anyone takes the knife out you have already left the building because your intuition is that strong. You can see the future unfolding in front of your eyes even before it has happened, your spirit guides warn you about every enemy and friend who is likely to backstab you. You can spot 'fake', 'flaky', 'lies' from a mile away and you don't give anyone a chance any more.

Because you are no longer getting delayed you will be able to give your all to whatever task you focus on. Whether it is talking about your own life, your life experience, your own childhood stories, how you have overcome huge struggles of your life, whether it is writing a book and telling your story or becoming a life coach, motivational speaker to heal millions of people all over the world. Whether it is about healing animals, or children or old sick lonely people. Whether it is about bringing the cosmic knowledge, cosmic codes through any form of channeling into creating the new earth or it is about spreading the love frequency all over the world by traveling wherever you go. It can be your art, your voice, your touch, your lifestyle or just your looks even which is very healing, freeing and transcending. It immediately takes another being to a different place, time or frequency. It can be many things, it is specific to your life, your abilities, your purpose, your karmic balance, what you owe to this world and you are very much aware of it by now. If you are still reading this book I am darn sure you are already living your purpose or are about to dive deep into it. Because you will read it till here only if it makes sense to you. Don't forget you are an old soul and you have come with a lot of wisdom and information already imprinted from your past incarnations, you are just integrating them into your current consciousness and unboxing all of those after your awakening. If I have to give an example, for someone to have a plethora of knowledge about all kinds of self healing modalities, cosmic channeling, astral ranks, supernatural strength, direct connection to ancestors and spirit guides, coding animal communication etc all at once is not possible unless they have mastered those skills in various other lifetimes and channeled and integrated them in this lifetime at this point. It is simply not possible otherwise for someone to have this sort of wisdom at a young age of a couple of decades. They have never learnt all those things here or hung around people who knew these skills in such a modern technological era. Where does all this information come from? It comes from your soul which is ancient. Your soul knows and remembers more than you think.

CHAPTER 8

CHOSEN ONES GET TRAINED IN THE ENEMY'S CAMP

You know how tough your life has always been right? Very challenging, full of hardships. And there will hardly be a Chosen One, I do not think there will be one who can confirm that their life was very easy without any hardships. I don't think there will be one who says they were born in regular functioning families with a regular upbringing. Maybe they went to the best schools and got the best education in their country but were compensated with other abusive and intense irregularities in the family. Born in a rich and privileged family does not make it a regular functioning family, a lot of times these royal, political and elite socially respected dynasties have huge dark secrets & dysfunctions hidden in their closets running from centuries. We have already discussed how a Chosen One's life is carefully designed by the Divine, thoughtfully weaved with experiences and events that leads them to their huge life purpose and blessed with the exact gifts and abilities which balance the karma of past lives etc.

We know by now that everything was designed by the universe, by God to appear in that way, to move in that manner because whatever your purpose is on this planet you will come to that realization at some point but first you must go through a certain sequence of events which will ultimately reveal yourself to you. Many Chosen Ones are still figuring out their missions, they're still figuring out why they are here, it takes time but time taken and properly used will reveal it all.

A lot of people might try to mislead you in another way by saying these things as conspiracy theories, some new age phenomena, or labels that someone has taught us online. But no this is the real deal, these are real experiences based on our real lives, of thousands of us, not one or two, that has led us to know who we are. They will try to block your development, stop you from knowing your real self, cut down your awakening by calling these things bluff and self proclaimed heroic labels. And if someone wants to stay in the old age, old way of thinking, doesn't want to free themselves then they have the free will to do so but I think there are many of us who are out growing that old age and we are starting to think for ourselves. If you're the person who wants to get stuck in those old dimensions and continue giving your power away then no one can blame you or help you. You can do what you want, you have got free will, but I would encourage you to think for yourself, not let others brainwash you and see if your life resonates with being a real Chosen One.

• THE REASON YOU ARE BROUGHT INTO THE CAMP / DARK CIRCUMSTANCES

There is a huge reason why the Divine puts the black sheeps in real traumatic and dark circumstances, it is for your training. Because God wants you to know how the enemy operates, yes my dear beloved God will place his chosen people in the Lion's Den, where the real battles take place. God wants you to learn the ways of the Devil, learn it so well that you can trick the negative energy when your time comes.

• CHOSEN ARE FAST LEARNERS, TAKING NOTE OF EVERYTHING

A chosen individual as they walk through life on a daily basis will be taking notes of every occurrence, they are very quick learners, who don't miss a chance to pick up practical lessons on the go. These traumatic environments which we call the Lion's Den have narcissists as well as the Chosen people, these environments are designed like that, like a game. The Chosen are literally getting trained in the Lion's den, acquiring new skills, remembering their lost abilities, sharpening their existing talents and understanding the entire game by playing it over and over again at various levels. Learning how to combat a new devil each time you level up, a stronger devil with complete unpredictability and superior danger. But you play the game well, you keep getting stronger, wiser, more street smart by getting hurt over and over again. You are also protected by the divine, they allow only that much pain that you can withstand. You are getting trained in a supervised arena but with a string attached to karma. Your opponents get karma each time they try to harm you, and similarly you get your good or bad karma depending on your intentions and actions. You level up, climb the ladder and receive the prizes faster than most people which is why you also become the target of everyone for envy and competition.

• IT COMES WITH THE TERRITORY

All the competition, jealousy and negative attention is part of the territory and can rarely be skipped. With time and experience you will be able to dodge, manage and ignore the negative attention as it comes, you will consider yourself as someone important who shows the mirror to anyone who comes in contact with you and invokes inspiration in some and throws light on their lack for some. Because remember there is always a balance of energies in the universe. Because you work with the divine, because you are surrounded by angels and divine beings that are constantly fueling you with positive cosmic energy you are naturally going to have to face some negativity too of equal thickness if not less. This continuous process of transmuting negative energy and remaining unfazed will keep you growing at a soul level, make you very powerful in spirit and flesh and also will stack up your arsenal. You are actually at the front line even without you knowing it, and all of the information picked up during the training will get used in various situations of life very unexpectedly and unpredictably. Sudden bubbles of information will keep popping in your head which will be exactly relevant to what you need at that moment. That is the divine and your angels coming through as intuition with what you need.

There will be a moment of your Awakening, it will arrive one fine day at some point in your life when you awaken to the truth of your existence, when you're going to understand what your life has always been about. And you will have a testimony to show because you've seen things and you've been in positions and places that nobody has been in. You must know by now that the people who go through the worst usually are the first ones to awaken. The people that go through the worst are God's chosen people and once they are nudged to speak about it they will say it all, they will give the testimony. They are going to say everything the way it is, pretty bluntly, they are not going to sugarcoat anything, they are going to keep it straight because they don't know any other way. They want to deliver the message the way they have received it without changing its frequency, without diluting its intensity.

• **THEIR TESTIMONIES ARE INTENSE**

The testimonies given by Chosen Ones will be very intense, sometimes they'll be talking about things deep from their childhood that will seem like a fairy tale, unbelievable stories. Let me tell you something, when you come close to a Chosen One, this mystery revolving around them and their life is undeniably obvious. You can see it, feel it and witness it because they have a testimony that nobody can believe, it is unbelievable when they start opening their mouth, when they start to speak you can barely believe what you are hearing. You will think the person is delusional and making up these stories because you cannot even fathom in your wildest dreams that a person has experienced so much and they are still here. They are still alive and thriving. They are healing even more, they are doing even better after everything they have gone through. That is the reason they tend to surprise their enemies, they have quite a few btw, like we have discussed a Chosen person has a lot of enemies ever since they were born. They are visible humans or sometimes hidden entities in energy form. But the way a Chosen rises out of their dirt and catastrophic situations each and every time they take their enemies by storm and dish them out big chunks of karma each time. They get frustrated as they never understand how you are still there, walking, talking and still thriving after they have done so much to you. To keep you from doing your work, from shining very bright and fulfilling your purpose. They have done so much to keep you under the mud and when they still see you rise they sometimes wonder if you are even human. Meanwhile the Chosen are doing better than what they used to do back in the day. Yes, a Chosen will have a very powerful testimony okay, but in those testimonies you are going to hear all kinds of dark stories, unbelievable, painful, trauma stricken stories which a normal person might not be comfortable with. But anyone, anybody who is on a spiritual journey, who is close to God, who is on a 'Chosen One' journey, will understand it completely, will want to hear these testimonies. Because the Chosen has got this Mission, a Divine Mission on this planet. How are they going to be able to execute their mission if they don't have a story?

• THE PRICE WAS HUGE AND HAS BEEN PAID

You have paid the price to learn deep secrets, understand all kinds of spiritual methods, and learnt how to play this 3D game well. Yes it has been very intense, the price has been huge too and God has revealed to you how the devil operates on this planet. How the enemy operates, how you have been swimming and diving with the enemy. When you are getting trained in the Enemy's camp, they think you are one of them. When they are playing their dirty mind games, hurting people, destroying others lives, ending someone's career, wishing someone's death they think you're one of them, they think you are with them like an ally. But once you leave the camp, after your training is done for that particular phase they will search for you desperately and try to bring you back. They won't believe what they see, they won't believe that they couldn't recognise you as an outsider. Their ego won't let them believe it for a long time. They will think you are faking it but once they really understand that you are actually not part of them but were there just to learn their ways they will feel highly betrayed. They will have a huge narcissistic injury and will now try to destroy your life. They will try to hunt you down, ruin whatever you have created and take everything good away from you. They won't be able to move on from it for years, they might put each and every resource they have only for your downfall. But they don't know you are the Chosen One and that all their efforts to hunt you will inevitably fail, they are only wasting all of their resources and precious time. With every attack you will only gain more wisdom, strength and faith. To be in the Lions Den for years is a huge price that the

Chosen One pays early in their childhood and throughout their life in various phases.

That is why when you come to these Chosen people you will find them narrating very very interesting stories which are very addictive sometimes. You will sit with them and you just want them to keep on talking and sharing their experiences because they will talk about stuff that you have only seen in movies or you have only read in fiction novels. But these are real plots and scenarios experienced by real people. They are giving testimonies of experiences a regular person can never even put together in their head.

CHAPTER 9

YOU ARE A WALKING TRIGGER, CHOSEN ONE

Chosen Ones by now you know number one you"e all about the truth and justice, number two you"e all about love and number three you"e all about being authentic. It doesn" necessarily mean chosen people are perfect, they have their own flaws too, they could be battling with their own issues but usually they are vibrating at the love frequency, they wear their authenticity, truth and justice as a cape and walk around. It may not have made a lot of sense way back in time but post awakening you are going to understand the reason why you have always been triggering people, the regular people you come into contact with on a daily basis, you trigger the hell out of them. They approach you with their fake smiles, their manipulation, their sly stories to get some dirt on you but you respond back with your blunt truth, a no nonsense attitude and refuse to play along in their energy. This triggers them bigtime and throws them off their seat, because they didn" expect you to see right through them, they don" know that you can judge their energy and know their intention even before they open their mouth. You can look into their soul through that flesh and bone they carry. They just can" fathom how you knew all of their intentions without even looking at them, they don" know the game of energy. They are not equipped enough to approach you because they learn the hard way that they need to come correct each and every time if they come to you at all. Gradually they figure out that you"e not going to be on their side anytime soon, they feel so powerless in front of you, none of their tricks work on you and that triggers them alot.

There are many people in this world who have never seen or felt love, never experienced genuine love their entire life. They don" know what it means or feels and the moment they come in contact with you they will get triggered bigtime. They will find your frequency very weird and difficult to stand in because you are at the love frequency whereby you actually can love somebody genuinely, you can love yourself unconditionally. You are love, your being is overflowing with love which is why you give it so easily, you don" hold it back, you don" think too much before giving it away, you have plenty of it within you and you are constantly getting replenished from the cosmos. Your talk and walk, so pure, your intentions straight to the point and your presence so unadulterated by the world that they will find it obnoxious. They will think there is something wrong with you, and try to find faults with you. But the truth is that they are getting triggered so much, they are feeling very hollow within and without, they are thinking to themselves how do beings like you even exist on earth. You see any time when you meet a person you are like a reflection of everything that they are not and they don" know what to do with you, they don" even know how to handle you. They feel very unequipped to deal with you while they thought they were very street smart in the 3D world and that triggers them furthermore into a spiral. You are going to trigger a lot of people everyday as you walk around in the streets, at work, in the supermarket etc. You don" have to do much, it" just your presence, your energy body holds a lot of high vibrational light, this light is going to intensively shine into their faces and they''e going to set off. You may see this, sometimes when a person all of a sudden gets irritated they might start talking by themselves, murmuring in their mouth while slyly looking at you from the side eye, they may start screaming insults at you out of nowhere, they may start throwing some shade at you and sometimes they may even physically try to attack you because they couldn'' handle your presence. There is a light that is shining all around you my dear Chosen Ones, and they cannot withstand this light. These people have been living in the dark for most of their lives, they''e been living in shame, they''e been living in hatred, in abuse, in spiritual prison and their soul is only used to that.

It can even happen in a very competitive atmosphere like a corporate job interview scenario, where you have got all the right qualifications, experience levels, even recommendations etc. It's almost as if you are overqualified for the job, where these employers should be grabbing you by your hand and offering you the best package but somehow nobody can hire you, for some reason the interviewers are going to desire to choose somebody else, someone who isn't that perfect for that position. That is because those people are already feeling a sense of threat, they know you are too smart and they might lose their own positions to you over the years. Or they might feel if they take you they will have to interact with you everyday and be reminded of everything that they are not, and that's not something they want to come across in their lives. So as you go along Chosen Ones you will experience meeting many individuals at different timelines of your reincarnation but for some reason people might walk away from you time and again.

YOU MUST KNOW HOW TO PROTECT YOUR-SELF WHEN YOU TRIGGER OTHERS

Which is why you must know how to protect yourself when you feel you are saying something that is irritating somebody, you must find the means to walk away from that situation if you perceive any danger beforehand, do not wait until things get out of hand. When you sense intense discomfort in their body language and expressions, you know they might verbally attack you or even try intimidating you physically, take quick measures at that point. Don't be afraid to call the law enforcement, call other people around you or just disappear very quick, protect yourself whichever way you need to.

You will trigger people everywhere you go, anywhere in this world by just showing up, and that is how you will know if you are a true Chosen One.

YOU HAVE NO ONE TO TALK TO OR CALL AND THEY REJECT YOU

HERE'S WHY!

- **YOU ARE AN ANOMALY**

When you are a Chosen One, throughout your life you will see that you are being ignored, put in a corner, kept at the back or not being valued for who you actually are by human entities. You might feel quite frustrated and never understand others' behaviour towards you, as to why you are being treated in that manner, why do people tend to unsee you or choose to leave you out. Why do people prefer others over you although you bring much more to the table than anyone else and are the better friend, employee, son/daughter etc. It is a very common life pattern in every Chosen One's journey and each one has gone through this. It happens because people around you can sense your power, your humongous potential while being around you. They can see your star power, the way your energy attracts people, how you turn every opportunity into a golden ticket and how fertile your land is. They get terrified observing this and get highly insecure around you. You as the Chosen One on the other hand are very humble and sometimes do not give yourself enough credit, which is why God has chosen your pure heart! The divine magnetic pure energy which you carry even you are unaware of, and hence they don't want to give you your well deserved flowers to keep you small. They think once you receive your accolades you will understand your value, become bigger than your surroundings and demand what you deserve. It's a similar situation like when you are the most charming, hardworking and intelligent employee and your boss knows it too but if he acknowledged that in you then he would have to pay you more so he would rather keep quiet. He is going to keep you exactly where you are and it's the same thing in real life in all kinds of relationships when you're dealing with people. They don't ever want you to realise your true potential, but they want to keep you around because they want to be in your orbit and act like you are nothing or not important in any way.

My dear Chosen you are everything and everybody knows it, everybody has seen glimpses of your magnificence so don't be fooled when people go around and act like they don't know who you are. A lot of times you just want to make friends like everybody else, you want to hang out with everybody else, you just want to kick it with everybody else and you wonder why doesn't anyone want to hang with you? Why don't you have any friends? Why can't you do the same things that everyone else does? Because you can't, because you're called to do something greater, you have to when you're chosen. You walk different, you move different, you do things differently than the average person does because you're just called to do something different and I know sometimes you want to feel like you're a part of the crowd. You want to be able to do what others are doing, go where they're going but you can't.

Have you ever noticed you are in a huge group of friends, with a bunch of people but you feel like an outsider, there are 15 people but you still feel alone. You might be in a relationship with somebody who is a great person but still feel like something is missing. You can be at a job where you are doing very well, earning big bucks, people respecting you even but still feel like you don't fit there, you are not exactly content. You might be married or be in your dream job and still feel like a loner, doing everything by the beat of your own drum, living in a certain space of your mind. That is because you are supposed to create a path of your own, you are not supposed to do just what you are told in a highly superficial profit based workplace. There are very few people like you all over the planet, far few in between. You are a leader and not a follower. But authorities everywhere, whether at the workplace or family will want to keep you away from your throne, so that you don't leave their lives. They want to keep you hidden because they don't want you to leave, because the truth is that they have never met anyone like you and never will and that's how you should feel about yourself too.

• YOU FORCE PEOPLE TO LOOK IN THE MIRROR

People want to water you down to the level that they are on, they want to water you down because when you enter a friend group you force people to come up and rise to the occasion. When you become friends with anyone they have no choice but to become a better person. You elevate everybody in your life, you raise everybody's temperature and they know it so they call you names, they might find you rude and arrogant, they might say they don't like you. All of this is because they know that you're better than them, they actually admire you in private but dislike you in public and if they had the opportunity they would live your life and even be you. If it was possible they would be very close to you, so that they could find out your life details and apply them to their life.

The thing is we don't know who we are, we don't know it to a huge extent because we allow people to treat us any type of way. We allow people to disrespect us because we don't know the extent of our uniqueness. If an eagle grew up with chickens all his life how will he know he's an eagle. When he's always been on the ground he will never know that he can soar in the sky, unless somebody comes and shows him who he truly is. And the best thing is you've had a season in your life where you figured out who you were real quick, due to some life events planned by the universe you figured out who you were in just a few years and you got to that point in your life where you finally gathered all the courage to put a stop to anything that was lesser than what you were and what you deserved.

Sometimes you must be wondering why your phones are not ringing, why we got these dry phones, nobody's calling us, we have no one to call either, no one to go out with, no one to hang out with, we do call people but they're not available and we're wondering why?! It's because you're Chosen, your life is marked for greatness and your season will come if it hasn't come already. It will come and you will know it, you will know what I am talking about. You will understand what I'm saying is real because your season will come. These people come to hurt you, disrespect you and make you feel like you're less than, that you're nobody, like they don't want to hang with you so they reject you. There are a lot of reasons for this, it's the universe's divine plans to open your eyes and your opponents' eyes in unexpected ways and unforeseen times. Just know that your eyes will be opened in this season and this is not the time to allow anyone to make you feel smaller than what you are because you're great.

At the end of the day as we move forward in this life we have to know and understand who we are, it doesn't matter if no one is calling you or you have no one to hang out with in some phases of your life. It's ok if you are not in a relationship and no one is asking you out. It's alright if you're rejected by your family, just know that everything is going to come full circle for you and you're going to be so thankful to know that you are in the right place at the right time.

When you are a Chosen, when your life is marked by the divine, then you don't have the right to live life on your own terms. **You live life on the terms of the divine.** What I mean by that is when you're called to do something great you can't just go out willy-nilly and kick it, you can't just go hang with anybody you wish, you can't just talk to anyone on the phone. You can't give your time and energy to just anyone who comes by. You will have to come to that acceptance that you are not meant to have a life like everyone else, do things that your peers do, have average dreams and settle down to what was handed to you. You're a brand and you have to look at yourself as that exclusive personal brand. Your energy is not to be easily attained or accessed because that way you will run out of your precious energy. You have done enough hanging out and over giving in the first phase of your life, now at this phase you must learn to withdraw. This is the season where you are growing, becoming better, doing more, trying to achieve more, aspiring to be great because you are great and a lot of times we water down who we are just to make others happy and keep the peace. But from now on you are not going to allow anyone to come into your life and water you down anymore.

You must understand that it is vice versa. People are not reaching out to you because you are also not reaching out to them energetically, you're elevating and they can sense it in your energy. They feel unwanted by you, they can see that you are moving upwards in your own league and you don't resonate with them anymore. They might not say it to you but they can surely see it, which is why they automatically will move out of your life. It is divinely orchestrated and is meant to happen in this manner. Things will be stripped out of your life as you are co creating with the divine and moving forward. Every Chosen goes through it. You must trust the process and I don't want you to give up just because you can't understand the whole sequence right now and you can't look into the future right now. I want you to understand that it's all designed to make you better, it's all designed to shape you into your greatness. You are on your way to greatness and at this point you don't have to wonder about the people you don't hear from. Things are looking like they are falling apart from the outside but actually when you go deeper you will see that things are actually falling together and I will tell you again it's all designed to make you better. You are the Chosen One after all, you will win, you will never lose because it's not designed for you to lose, it's designed for you to win every single time and you must know and believe that on your journey throughout your life.

As you're on your journey everything good, noble and everything beautiful is coming to you and everything in your life that you do not need is being stripped away, all the unwanted and outgrown layers are being stripped away off of you and out of your life. You're coming out of your shell, it's a transfiguration, a whole transfiguration of you becoming the person that you've always aspired to be, you're becoming the person that you've always been called to be. As Chosen Ones we must know that everytime we walk away from any situation 'the way' is being made for us, every single time we are moving forward we are charting a path forward and are not looking back ever. And about all the things happening in your life you're basically quieting the noise around you, (it's all absurd noise by the way trying to distract you and keep you from your highest potential), you're not listening to it because this is not the season for you to lose your mind, this is the season for you to remain grounded. Everyone knows who you are but the question is do you know who you are! Right now your phone is dry and no one's calling but when your season comes everyone's going to call you, everything in your life that you think you lost will come back, every person, every situation, every opportunity. Everything is working out for you, it's all coming together for you, you have to know it and you have to trust it. You have to move like **'the greats'**, you're great, you have the energy of the greats and hence you must move and live your life as greatness.

NEW LEVELS, NEW DEVILS

It's not the time for you to concern yourself with what they're saying or doing, remember these agents of the universal negative energy will always exist in one form or another. Either as family or friends, either as hateful obsessive ex's or hateful ex colleagues, either as online trolls or low vibrating neighbours. It is the balance of the universe, because you are a beacon of light, the negative forces will always be attracted to you, try to attack you and delay your mission. The higher levels of ascension you reach you will be met with higher negative forces. It's the saying, **'New levels, New Devils'**. So now that you know these devils are always going to be there, look at them as catapulting tools, you must just use them to push yourself forward in your journey. Transmute the negative energy projected by them as fuel and use it to reach your goals faster. Instead of getting angry or reacting in the same energy as them, use that to fuel yourself. It is time for you to move forward in your life and pursue your mission, without bothering about your surroundings.

CHAPTER 10

ADVANCED SIGNS

AS YOU ANSWER YOUR CALLING AND WALK YOUR PATH

ARE YOU A CHOSEN ONE?

Who is a Chosen One and what does it really mean to be a Chosen One? Many people tend to mistake it with personality traits. Personality traits have nothing to do with being a Chosen One. Being an introvert or self sufficient, intuitive doesn't make one to be a Chosen, although they are parts of the qualities of being a Chosen. A Chosen One is a person who has been ordained by the universe to serve a far greater purpose for all humanity. They are the soldiers of the Most High, walking on the surface of the earth in human form. Of course, Chosen people accepted to be born into this realm, at this time on planet Earth so as to carry out their significant assignments for the universe. Sometimes knowing you're a Chosen One is difficult as being told straight up that you're on a very unique journey and you are destined for greatness. However, getting to know you're the Chosen One means picking up on slight clues gradually and slowly coming to terms with the truth that you're the King or Queen who was sworn or the one who was anointed. It is time to wake the Chosen Ones up and know who they truly are. These are some signs that you might resonate with. Some of you might relate with all or most of these situations.

1. YOU WERE ALMOST UNALIVED

So the first sign that usually happens to most Chosen people is that you are almost unalived (killed) at some point in life. Usually this happens at an early age. We see the story of Moses. We see the story of Jesus. In their cases there was some type of decree that went out which was purposely put there to kill them at a very early age. The enemy is not going to be happy with your huge calling and enormous destiny. He's going to try to take you out at an early age. So think back to when you were a kid. Usually this is going to happen between the age of one or ten years old. An example would be if someone was a product of rape, where they were going to get aborted as a foetus before their birth itself but was allowed to live and given a life after consultation and agreement with the rape victim. It can also be something really terrible that happened in your life which led to a near death experience. Every Chosen One has experienced one or more terrible things as a little child, teenager and even adult. Because of this unique mission of the Chosen Ones to raise the vibration of the Earth, they are often stricken with hardship, horrible accidents and so on. Everything is metaphysical. These kinds of people have a divine mark in their physical or even spiritual body which is noticed and watched by the evil spirits and different kinds of negative energies. Chosen people face a lot of obstructions, tribulations on their way of success for no reason. What others tend to achieve easily, the Chosen Ones work twice as hard and struggle with it even harder in life. This is not because they are not intelligent enough to get to their goals in life, but because they are tracked and blocked on purpose by the evil spirits.

2. SEPARATION FROM FAMILY

You went through some type of family separation. Now, this could happen with your physical family, or with a group of close friends in your life. Everybody's going to have a different situation, take it as it resonates but this situation was to isolate you. Now, sometimes this is actually a good benefit if you are Chosen. The reason why you're getting separated from your family is so that God can actually begin to talk to you, begin to minister to you, can start doing the spiritual work with you, to show you how to use the gift that you're called to give to this world and how to use your light. He's going to be training you during this separation period so that you can go ahead and bring what you're supposed to bring to the world. So that you can give birth to what you are destined to.

3. EXTREME HARDSHIP

You went through extreme hardships. It will be different for different situations. For example, I also experienced molestation in college by my local guardian while doing some project work at his place. He was as old as my Dad, I trusted him but he took advantage of my vulnerable situation and young age. More examples can be someone growing up in a household where they had to deal with molestation or rape on a regular basis by a family member. Or someone who grew up in extreme poverty, with no education until a certain age. Something severe happened to you, maybe a bad incident which broke your confidence and took years to heal and recover. And these things were there to scare you and stop you from moving forward with your purpose that God has chosen for you.

4. YOU ARE HATED AND LOVED FOR NO REA-SON

This one should resonate with any person who is Chosen. You can't understand it. You can't explain it. You are hated for no reason and loved for no reason. Everything is energy which comprises positivity and negativity. People in this world today tend to hate the Chosen Ones not because they are haters or evil, but because bad spirits and entities have taken possession of their bodies which manipulates them to do so. They don't even know that they are possessed. You will walk into a room with people, and again, for the most part, most people will be nice to you. But there's somebody hanging around that's hating on you. There are people that would hate you although you are a good person, you are a genuine person. You try to uplift people and the society in general but for whatever reason, some people just can't stand you without a reason. There's barely any logic to it, if you ask them they won't be able to put a finger on answering the 'why?', they won't be able to give you any good reason for why they don't like them so much. And that's because people can see your light, your light always bothers them. You have so many gifts that God has given you, that He wants to give birth through you, and it's like something inside of them that is just fighting against that light of yours. It wants to throw stones at you so that you get distracted from your purpose and fall off your divine path and journey. There is so much going on in this reality beyond what the eyes can perceive. These kinds of people always vibrate with a low frequency of hate, lack, jealousy, shame and anger. On the other hand many people love to stay around the Chosen Ones due to their very high positive state of vibration.

They also attract a lot of positive high vibration people around them as they effortlessly make people happy. Their positive aura revitalises other people's life, makes them feel blessed and that is why many people keep gravitating towards their field of energy knowingly or unknowingly. It could be difficult to figure out why people love you so much, especially when there is no reason for that. This is because you are chosen by the Most High to raise the vibration of this realm.

5. YOU USE YOUR INTUITION AS YOUR INNER GUARD

Chosen people are very intuitive and psychic in nature. Your intuition is your inner guard. There is that inner clock sensor or switch which gives you signals in different ways, through your dreams, through synchronicities, through the inner voice suddenly whispering giving instructions, sudden change in your emotions when you come to spaces, by the ringing of ears, by your eyeballs movement etc. You are always aware and tend to know when something is about to start, stop or happen. This is because your third eye is always active, watching through the lies and deceit of everyone around you, of the society. It is very hard to fool a Chosen One, especially in friendships, family and romantic relationships. Your third eye is open and you already know that no one can lie to you through your intuition, you know very well when one is being fake or real, true or false.

6. ALL EYES ARE ON YOU, LIKE A TARGET

Everywhere you go, it feels like all eyes are on you, as if you are targeted. This is one of the most difficult parts of being a Chosen One. No one can stand being a target for no reason in society. You walk into a room, people start looking at you as if something is written on your forehead. However, these are actually not people looking at you, they are invisible forces or spirits who are watching you through the eyes of men and women you encounter on a daily basis. They might be planning how to suck away your energy or ask for your valuable information so that they can latch on to your energy. So make sure to protect your energy, your workplace and living place with an intention, prayer etc.

7. YOU NEVER TRULY FIT IN

Like we have spoken about it earlier in this book, Chosen Ones never truly fit in anywhere even if they try to. They will always stand out even amongst the rebels and various groups of people who are social misfits. You may have been an outcast, a very popular loner, where even this popularity gains momentum because of your lone wolf mysterious outsider personality. You may have been 'the black sheep' in your family where you just never felt like you had a place you could call home. It was just a place you went back everyday after school and work but you couldn't get the feeling of home, because the true 'home' is nowhere else but in 'YOU'. YOU are your 'HOME'. Wherever you go you make it home, it is beyond the geographical or familiar understanding, it is about your energy, your true authentic undisturbed essence that makes any space 'HOME'. A lot of people will want to hang out with you ofcourse, they will want to experience your energy while offering you many things, trying to make deals with you, but none of that entices you, because you want to just rush back to your home, to your sacred safe space enriched with divine guidance and abundance which is you. You value being by yourself, you experience divine bliss in it and you can hardly explain it to anyone, and which is why you just accept the fact that you are not meant to fit in, you are meant to stand out at all times in all circumstances by default.

You don't fit into any system and can be very rebellious in nature. You question everything and never try to follow anybody or any institute. When society says do this, you prefer to do the opposite. This rare group of people are always thirsting for pure knowledge of the universe. As the society is moving in one direction like flocks of sheep, Chosen people go the other direction, researching and questioning the system of societal norms and traditions. You always follow the voice of your heart and you do not like moving an inch without connecting with your mind and your heart. You always know that there is something wrong with this society. You know you are the spirit having a human experience. You believe in the equality of everything in existence. You know you are one with the universe and there is no difference between you and other life forms. So therefore you give equal respect to everything in existence.

8. YOU ARE A HERMIT MOST OF THE TIME

As a Chosen One, you prefer to live alone in truth than to live in deceit and lies like the masses. This is not because you don't know how to deal with people, not at all. Chosen Ones are masters in handling different kinds of people and even difficult situations in their lives. They choose to stay alone because they are often misunderstood, hated by many in society. How is it even possible to understand or love someone who lives in a totally different frequency? People cannot fathom what it is like to live at a different frequency. And that is what makes it very difficult to deal with a Chosen One. This set of people tend to spend a lot of time alone meditating and connecting themselves back to the universe after having spread a lot of love and positive energy around other people. They need time to rejuvenate themselves and divinely connect back to the infinite realm of consciousness from where they get their sacred wisdom and knowledge. This is why many people see you as hyper intelligent, because you are full of natural intelligence. Many people tend to gravitate more towards you to seek more sacred knowledge.

You will lose friends, companions and partners when God calls you, don't be surprised if your friends start leaving you. You might find out that people you used to hangout with just don't seem to understand you anymore. But the truth is, when God calls you, you will start to see things differently and your priorities will shift. You'll remove them because He doesn't want anyone to be a hindrance to your calling. In fact, even if he doesn't remove them, you might find out that they are starting to leave on their own. This is because the light in you convicts them of the darkness in them. So if you're going through this right now, don't let it get you down.

9. SOMEONE WHO'S CHOSEN WILL TELL YOU THAT YOU ARE ALSO ONE

So, I came to know about myself through all kinds of Chosen One content that I came across in the last 5 years, everywhere. Through various mediums, not just Youtube, but through books, through podcasts on other platforms. The specific angel numbers which are for the Chosen Ones started appearing in front of my eyes everywhere I went, because I was aligning and believing that about myself more and more. All these content videos, readings, testimonies and rite of passage messages were given to me by the universe at that time. So for me it was not one person but a collective of Chosen Ones whose content I came across and I understood that about me. There were way too many similarities in the life stories and patterns of theirs to mine where even if I didn't believe it initially, I was thrown down more holes and passages of this awakening, given more time and divinely orchestrated good and bad events kept unfolding which forced me to learn about myself. I was even informed that if I didn't learn and accept my destiny as a Chosen One I would be at a great loss, I would create further negative karma for myself as that would mean I am rejecting the enormous gifts that are given to me in this lifetime and wasting them. And that even if I have been using other talents to make a living and earn a name, I still won't be reaching the peak of my Abundance in every aspect of my life unless I use the specific gifts to share my wisdom, help the community and change the world with the example of my own life experience. It's like some gifts and talents get activated at certain times and phases in your life, when you are confident enough to use it, when you believe in it very strongly inside and out. It will all align together, you will be ready and the world also will be ready to hear it, that is when they are activated in you. And at that phase we must use those gifts and not waste them. So, for me it was very clear and I decided to write this book, so that it can reach potential Chosen Ones all over the world. I will be activating the 144 dna in many people through this book. You might start seeing the angel number 144 everywhere from now on. It is a dedicated angel number for Chosen Ones. You were guided to read this book for a reason, the universe has brought it to you, right. I believe that you are Chosen and God wants to activate you and do something incredible in your life.

10. GOD, SOURCE, UNIVERSE HIMSELF WILL CONFIRM YOU ARE A CHOSEN ONE

Whatever you believe in, however you call it, in whichever way you connect with 'IT'. GOD, Source, the Universe, divine energies that you connect with, cosmic entities that you collaborate with or religious deities that you worship, in whichever way you experience divinity, at some point in your life it will speak back to you with confirmation. Not one, not two but many confirmations will be sent your way just so that you don't miss it. They will confirm it as many times as you need to believe in it. They will also show you which path, what kind of journey and ultimately what work you are meant to do as a Chosen. Which sector of life, which industry and what kind of community you are going to affect with your abilities. What kind of patterns you will break and how you will change your immediate environment. You will be used as an instrument, as a vehicle to bring change into the world through step by step divine guidance. Which is why a lot of sensitivity and faith will be brought into you during your isolation, psychic powers and intuitive abilities will be heightened by the divine as you get into your regular spiritual practices so that you can hear what GOD is saying. So that you can spot the signs and signals when they are shown to you, so that every synchronicity is not lost in the madness of the matrix and you gradually come into alignment with the GOD codes and your Higher self.

Whatever you went through and overcame in your life, all the patterns that you broke, they can be multiple things, emotional even physical and multiple generational curses too. Pay close attention to it. Maybe it was some type of abuse as a child, surviving trauma from an extremely difficult narcissistic parent, depression, severe bullying in school or teenage relationship trauma, physical health issues or anything. In 9 out of 10 cases, whatever that big traumatic experience a Chosen One was able to overcome with the help of the divine, that is what they are meant to help other people with. Because they have gotten so good at dealing with a certain specific pattern by having gone through it deeply and dealing with it over and over again, a Chosen gets multiple degrees in it. They attain mastery with researching, analysing, and solving the case with their extreme expertise, and hence are Chosen by the divine to help others find solutions in that same segment of trauma. It is that specific calling to help save other people who are about to hit that situation or have just entered the cycle.

11. AN INSATIABLE HUNGER FOR RIGHT-EOUSNESS

One of the most apparent signs God has called you is that you will have an unquenchable desire for the things of God. This is because when God calls you, his primary aim will be to renew your spirit. This will lead to you having a strong zeal and hunger for the things of God. Jesus said blessed are they that hunger after righteousness, for their cup shall always be filled by the Divine. You might discover that you start to feel a sudden urge to read the Bible, listen to sermons, chant mantras, sit in Sadhana or interact with other believers and take active part in the spiritual community. You might want to dig for more information about your ancestry, learn about your bloodline, get to know about your birth chart so that you strengthen yourself with the right remedies etc. And the most important thing is you don't leave any opportunity to do good for others, whether it's humans or animals. You have deep compassion for every being and go out of your way to heal and help them as your own. This isn't just a passing interest, it's a deep burning desire that you can't ignore. The reason God will do this is because he wants to fill your spirit by equipping you with the knowledge and power you need, by making you do a lot of good karma so that it can attract more blessings and abundance in return which can help you further in your purposeful journey. And point No 9 is an extension to this divine degree of righteousness.

This will cause you to have no tolerance for injustice and unright-eousness. When you have such a strong conviction, you will feel compelled to stand against evil. In many cases, God will want you to advocate on behalf of others who cannot do so themselves. This will involve standing up for the voiceless or speaking out against oppression. You will be moved by a desire to protect and defend those who cannot fight for themselves. You will even be willing to take risks in order to champion the cause of righteousness and speak out against unrighteousness.

12. YOU SEE DIVINITY AND GOOD IN EVERY-BODY AND EVERYTHING

Though this can be strange for many people since it is not how the societal ego and system was constructed. You don't look down on anybody and you prefer to respect all life forms. Most of the Chosen Ones are now realising how important it is to protect all kinds of animals, just like the Ancients did. If you are now realising this or having any little intuition about the universal unity in existence, know that you are a Chosen One who just needs to wake up. Everything is divine and divinely connected. The cry of an animal being slaughtered isn't different from the cry of man when being slaughtered as well. We are all forms of energy vibrating in different frequencies. I speak and understand human languages through the same universal consciousness. I experience life, therefore I am. On the other hand, all other animals speak and understand animal languages through the same universal consciousness. They experience life, therefore they exist, therefore they are. All life forms are ONE, from the same divine consciousness, the Creator. And therefore no one has the right to take the life or freedom of another being. This has always been in the mindset of the chosen people of this planet, which will definitely prevail with time.

13. YOU EASILY FEEL CONVICTED WHEN GOD CALLS YOU

Another obvious sign you notice will be that you will always feel convicted whenever you do something wrong. Let me explain, when God calls you, the first thing he does is to separate you from the nature of sin. So whenever you do something sinful, your conscience will come alive and you will immediately have a sense of regret each time you do something wrong. It means that the Spirit of God is actively trying to purge you and help you become a clean person. When individuals feel a divine calling, the contrast between that calling and their actions can create a heightened sense of conviction when they commit a sin. This inner conflict often stems from an acute awareness of their moral and spiritual obligations, making any deviation from their values feel particularly poignant. A regular person won't feel uneasy or experience sleepless nights after doing anything wrong, they won't even hold themselves responsible for that action. They will be entitled to their behaviour and will remain regret free. For those who believe they are guided by a higher purpose, straying from that path can trigger feelings of guilt and remorse. The sense that they are falling short of the expectations associated with their calling can amplify these emotions, leading to a deeper introspection about their choices and behaviour.

Moreover, this conviction can serve as a catalyst for personal growth and transformation. The discomfort that arises from sinning in light of a divine calling often compels you to reassess your actions and seek reconciliation. You will find that these moments of conviction prompt you to engage in prayer, seek forgiveness, or recommit to your spiritual journey. While the experience can be painful, it can also lead to a renewed dedication to living in accordance with your faith, ultimately fostering a stronger relationship with God and a clearer understanding of your path.

14. YOU FEEL A SENSE OF RESPONSIBILITY TO WAKE PEOPLE UP

This is because you have awakened to the true Divine Consciousness, and therefore you have many responsibilities to awaken the unawakened and guide them towards the righteous aspect of life. That is the most important responsibility of the Chosen Ones. Though your messages, your knowledge and wisdom may appear weird to many people around you, that is because they are not in the same frequency of consciousness as you. You always find yourself trying to push people towards the way of righteousness, but they often run away from you. This is because you are divinely selected by the Universe. You have the inner strength and desire to offer help to strangers, friends and even those who have wronged you. How many times do you find yourself helping people over and over again? How many times do you try to tell people the truth about this world? But they always see it as a conspiracy theory. Of course, many people will take longer to catch up with your wisdom nevertheless, no matter what happens, be on your divine path and keep on doing the work that has been assigned to you by the universe.

15. TRIALS AND TEMPTATIONS WILL AMPLIFY TO DISTRACT YOU

An obvious sign that shows that God has called you is that you will face an incredible amount of temptation. Many people mistakenly assume temptations to suddenly stop once God calls them. This is a false belief. In fact, if earlier you were only tempted ten times a day, now your level of trials and temptations will increase by 100 times a day. God's calling upon your life doesn't mean the devil will leave you alone. In fact, you will face the highest levels of temptation you've ever faced, the devil will intensify. This is so that you get overwhelmed and discouraged. If you must serve God, you must be prepared for times when you will be tempted. In fact, people who never used to offend you before will suddenly start to get on your nerves. This will be the period in which your calling and standing with God will be tested. But you should not be afraid to face temptations, rather you should be confident to confront them, knowing God is more than able to deliver you from all manners of temptations.

16. YOU WILL BE FILLED WITH DIVINE AUTHORITY

When God calls you, he will bestow a lot of power upon you. This power that will come from above will be accompanied by a high level of authority. Now, this authority doesn't mean you will boss people around or make demands. It's a different kind of authority, one that comes from humility and grace. This means you might find yourself doing things you normally won't do. From time to time, you might wake up and suddenly find yourself feeling like preaching or praying for someone. The Divine will begin to move you just like he moved the apostles. You won't be in control of yourself. You might see a sick person and you find yourself laying hands on them to pray for them. You won't know why you are doing this, how are you feeling unconditional compassion for everyone around you but you will just have that authority from above. Naturally, you might be very shy in real life, but when God calls you, you will find your forwardness. You will become very bold and full of wizardry. You could stand in front of large crowds and speak to all classes of people without feeling afraid. In the Holy books, every time God called anyone, he spent time encouraging them to be bold and not carry fear.

17. YOUR GLORY ALSO ATTRACTS PERSECUTION AND DISCRIMINATION

God's calling comes with glory. But that glory also attracts adversity. When you sign up to be a God's representative, you're signing up for a life of persecution. You're signing up for the life of someone who is going to be criticised and judged. People who knew you might be the first to look down on you. They might even threaten to cut off ties with you. Sometimes, God might be using you in ways that others haven't seen, and so they will be the first to rise up against you, telling you that you aren't of God. But don't let that discourage you. Remember, you're not doing this for them. You're doing this because you feel a calling that's bigger than yourself. Persecution is not a sign of weakness, it's a sign of strength. When you're called by God, you'll have the strength to face whatever comes your way. You'll have the courage to stand by your beliefs even when others don't agree with you. In fact, if in your calling you don't face persecution, you should really be concerned because everyone called by God will experience some level of harassment and oppression.

This is a reality that underscores the complex relationship between divine purpose and societal response. Their commitment to living a life of faith and integrity frequently challenges established norms and confronts the status quo, provoking reactions from those who may feel threatened by their values. This persecution can manifest in various forms, from verbal criticism to social ostracism, and even violent opposition. Yet, for many spiritual individuals, these trials serve as a testament to their faith and dedication to God's glory, illustrating the saying that 'with great power comes great responsibility'. The resistance they face often reinforces their sense of purpose, prompting them to stand firm in their beliefs and to embody the very values that attract such challenges.

Moreover, the discrimination faced by these Chosen Ones can serve as a catalyst for growth, both personally and within their communities. Enduring hardship often strengthens their resolve, allowing them to cultivate resilience and empathy, which can inspire others. As they navigate the complexities of persecution, these individuals may also become beacons of hope for those who share similar struggles. Their experiences can foster a deeper understanding of the divine, showing how adversity can be intertwined with spiritual growth and transformation. In this way, the persecution they face is not just an obstacle but a profound opportunity to reflect God's glory, manifesting in acts of love and compassion that challenge hate and division. Ultimately, their journey highlights the reality that true spiritual strength often emerges in the face of adversity, affirming their role as catalysts for change and ambassadors of divine love in a world that sometimes resists it.

18. GUIDANCE THROUGH DIVINE DREAMS AND VISIONS

Spiritual individuals Chosen by God often experience divine dreams that serve as powerful indicators of their significant life purpose and destiny. These dreams can manifest as vivid visions, symbolic messages, or profound insights that resonate deeply with their soul. Many spiritual traditions suggest that such dreams are not mere figments of imagination, rather, they are a form of guidance from a higher power, illuminating a path that aligns with their true calling. In these moments of deep connection, the dreamers may receive clarity about their roles in the world, be it through service, leadership, or creative expression, reinforcing the belief that they are part of a grand divine plan.

Moreover, these dreams often carry transformative messages that inspire individuals to embrace their unique gifts and talents. They may find themselves motivated to take bold steps toward fulfilling their destiny, supported by a sense of divine assurance that they are not alone in their journey. The recurring themes in these dreams can highlight core values, such as love, compassion, and wisdom, encouraging the dreamers to embody these principles in their waking lives. As they navigate challenges and opportunities, the dreams serve as beacons of hope and direction, reminding them of their inherent worth and the profound impact they are destined to make in the world. Thus, the interplay between divine dreams and spiritual calling underscores the belief that every individual has a significant purpose woven into the fabric of existence, waiting to be discovered and realised.

The divine can tell you through dreams and visions that He has called you. For instance, you might dream and see yourself preaching to a large crowd or leading a crowd in praise and worship. This is an indication that God is calling you into service. You might also find yourself regularly having dreams of various revelations, recurring dreams of certain celebrities who are indicating a certain manifestation skill or life path. Sometimes you see different versions of yourself, basically you come from other dimensions to give yourself relevant advice and ideas that you need at that point. This means the spirit of God is ministering to you. Or you might even dream of seeing angelic visitations. Or you find yourself performing miracles in the dream. All these are indications that God has chosen you.

19. YOU WILL BE GOD CONSCIOUS, AS IN CONSCIOUS OF GOD'S PRESENCE

Another and the final key that we are talking about in this book is that you will become very God conscious. You will have a constant sense of God's Presence around you and in everything you do. You will constantly keep thinking of God's opinion about it, you will no longer do things independently as you used to do before. It means that you will be constantly aware of God's presence around your life and will always seek to align your thoughts and actions with His will. You will be less concerned about your own desires and wants and more focused on serving the greater good and doing what is right in God's eyes, you will weigh your options more carefully and consider how each choice aligns with God's plan for your life. You will also find that your relationships with others are impacted in a positive way as you strive to be more kind, compassionate and forgiving, just as God would want you to be.

This divine consciousness permeates their thoughts, actions, and daily lives. This deep awareness stems from their recognition of a divine calling that goes beyond mere existence. It compels them to seek a relationship with God that informs their choices and priorities. As they cultivate this connection, they become more attuned to the presence of the divine in every aspect of their lives, viewing ordinary moments as opportunities for spiritual growth. This heightened awareness fosters a sense of responsibility to live in alignment with their faith, guiding them to embody principles such as love, compassion, and integrity in their interactions with others.

Their spiritual practices not only deepen their understanding of God's will but also enhance their ability to discern the divine in the world around them. As they grow in this consciousness, they may also feel a compelling urge to serve others, recognizing that their spiritual gifts are meant to contribute to the greater good. This commitment to service often results in transformative actions that inspire those around them, creating a ripple effect of spiritual awareness and compassion in their communities. In essence, the journey of being chosen by God cultivates a profound God consciousness that guides individuals in their quest for purpose, shaping their identities as they navigate the complexities of life with faith and grace.

BIBLIOGRAPHY

https://www.wikihow.com/Black-Sheep-of-the-Family#:~:tex t=Black%20sheep%20are%20people%20who,sad%2C%20lone ly%2C%20or%20unworthy.

https://www.youtube.com/watch?v=teJWQdT_Gw

https://www.biblekeeper.com/signs-you-are-chosen-by-god/

https://lonerwolf.com/black-sheep-of-the-family/

https://www.psychologytoday.com/us/blog/making-the-who le-beautiful/202201/the-lighter-and-shadowy-sides-being-the -black-sheep

https://www.prospecttherapy.com/blog/2018/6/12/how-bei ng-the-black-sheep-of-your-family-affects-your-mental-health

https://www.psychologytoday.com/us/blog/making-the-who le-beautiful/202201/the-lighter-and-shadowy-sides-being-the -black-sheep

https://medium.com/invisible-illness/the-black-sheep-how-y ou-can-help-8b2204955b2b

https://www.anniewright.com/the-power-of-being-the-black-sheep-in-your-family/

https://www.psychologytoday.com/intl/blog/invisible-bruises/202304/are-you-the-family-black-sheep-heres-how-to-deal

https://www.youtube.com/watch?v=MTJ6ymdsWxw

https://www.youtube.com/watch?v=LrmTTJEdV8o

https://www.youtube.com/watch?v=za3f9uj0Dok

MAY I ASK YOU FOR A SMALL FAVOR?

I want to express my sincere gratitude for choosing to invest your time in reading this book. Your decision to explore this work among countless others means a lot to me.

I hope that within these pages, you've discovered actionable insights that can enhance your daily life. Your journey doesn't have to end here, though.

May I kindly request an additional 30 seconds of your valuable time?

Sharing your thoughts about the book through a review would be immensely appreciated. Your review serves as a beacon, guiding other readers to take a chance on my books. It's a small gesture that carries significant weight in the world of authors.

To submit your review effortlessly, please scan the below **QR Code**. It will take you directly to the book's review page:

"I AM THE CHOSEN ONE"

Alternatively, you can also find the "**Reviews Section**" of this book's page on Amazon.

Your review will require just a minute of your time but will make a monumental difference in helping me connect with a broader audience and I eagerly look forward to reading your review.

Once again, thank you for your unwavering support of my work.

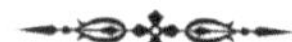

DISCLAIMER

This book is for educational purposes only. Readers acknowledge that the author does not render legal, financial, medical, or professional advice. The content within this book has been derived from various sources. Please consult a licensed professional before attempting any techniques outlined in this book.

By reading this document, the reader agrees that under no circumstances is the author responsible for any direct or indirect losses incurred as a result of the use of the information contained within this document, including but not limited to errors, omissions, or inaccuracies.

Adherence to all applicable laws and regulations, including international, federal, state, and local governing professional licensing, business practices, advertising, and all other jurisdictions, is the sole responsibility of the purchaser or reader.

Neither the author nor the publisher assumes any responsibility or liability whatsoever on behalf of the purchaser or reader of these materials. Any perceived slight of any individual or organization is purely unintentional.